The Bairn

A Cullercoats Childhood

Elaine Whitesides

North Tyneside Council

First co-published 2006 by IRON Press
and North Tyneside Libraries and Museums
IRON Press, 5 Marden Terrace, Cullercoats
Northumberland, NE30 4PD
tel/fax: +44 (0)191 253 1901
ironpress@blueyonder.co.uk
www.ironpress.co.uk

North Tyneside Libraries and Museums
Central Library, Northumberland Square
North Shields, NE30 1QU

ISBN 0 906228 94 8

Printed by Aeroprinting
Jarrow, Tyneside

FIRST EDITION

Typeset in Times New Roman 10pt

Cover artwork by David McConochie

IRON Press books
are distributed by Central Books
and represented by Inpress Limited,
Northumberland House,
11 The Pavement, Pope's Lane,
Ealing, London W5 4NG
Tel: +44 (0)20 8832 7464
Fax: +44 (0)20 8832 7465
www.inpressbooks.co.uk

Photo by Derek Whitehouse, Melton Mowbray

Elaine Whitesides

Having left Cullercoats for the University of Nottingham at the age of eighteen, Elaine Whitesides spent the greater part of her unremarkable life teaching English in the East Midlands. In recent years she has found that her true vocation is retirement. The important things in her life include two sons, two stepdaughters, and an increasing number of grandchildren living in various parts of the world. This necessitates frequent travel, a stimulating mixture of nervous flying and love of exotic places. When she is at home she is studying for a degree in Opera Studies and offers consultancy in stress management at a nearby health hydro.

This book is dedicated to the memory
James and Winifred Hull

The Bairn

Early
Memories

My mother and I went to the doctor together. I was three years old, it was a Spring day, April probably, and a shaft of pale yellow light was mysteriously balanced across the gloom of the waiting room. I watched slowly floating motes drift in and out of its spot-light, fascinated in a dreamy hypnotic way by their tiny flights. If I could see one of them closely enough, would it turn out to be a gauzy-winged fairy with curly hair and an artistically ragged dress made of shreds of rainbow like the ones in my story book?

The room was quiet, the atmosphere pervaded with a sense of patience. In those days (it was 1949), you did not make an appointment to see the doctor. The surgery was open for a time in the morning and again in the evening, and in between he came to your house. So the five or six other people sitting in the gloom around the slanting column of light waited, sitting decorously, occasionally breaking the silence with a shuffle or cough. One woman sitting opposite me wore high-heeled shoes and a chain around her ankle. Somehow I knew this made her a person that my mother would not know. I imagined that if she went in for her consultation ahead of us, the doctor would have to give the room a quick spray with something smelling of disinfectant before we went in. This was how our own home was kept in a state of grace.

After a while it was our turn. This caused me a mild flutter of excitement and nervousness. My health had not been good recently, so I associated Dr. Yeoman with the symptoms of whooping cough and the sense of reliance and reassurance that had come with recovery under his supervision. In my memory he is a big dark-haired bear of a man, with a loud, confident voice, the big accentless voice that denoted education, status, a position in life separate from others, but also familiar and comforting.

On this occasion, however, the consultation hardly involved me. I sat swinging my legs on a chair in the corner until the business was over. Then my mother gave me a penny, the large brown coin with the picture of a helmeted and robed figure moulded on one side. I was familiar with this image because it was my favourite to make by scribbling. This involved placing the coin under a piece of paper and rubbing over it with a pencil until the picture came through. Like brass-rubbing but smaller. I was instructed to give the coin to Dr. Yeoman 'for the baby'. This moment of memory confirms my smallness. In my mind's eye, he popped his head over a dark screen of polished wood topped with a band of ornately carved trellis. Years later I described this memory to my mother, and she shook her head doubtfully. No, there had not been a wooden screen in the surgery. Then she remembered; the doctor's desk was a dark polished mahogany with a carved galleried edge. So as I handed over the penny which was to buy me a brother, I was shorter than the height of the desk.

I find this memory interesting. Was it a tradition or superstition that required an existing child to buy the safe passage of the next one, or was it an exercise in child psychology? It seems that I was being encouraged to take on some personal involvement or ownership in this coming baby, probably to avoid jealousy and consequent misbehaviour on my part. The gesture was wasted in every respect. For a start, I had no idea which baby was being referred to, and in any case, although the question of the origin of babies had not yet occurred to me, I knew instinctively that they were not bought with pennies in the doctor's surgery, like an item of grocery. Then again, jealousy was not to be avoided in that way. He became known for his beauty and good temper, and he was younger than I, and smaller for quite a long time, so expectations were without rigour, and affection lavished upon him. Above all, he was a boy, which conferred a mysterious element of tragic importance. Was this a phenomenon of a post-war world, which had taken on an attitude of mind in which little boys were somehow regarded as the material for potential grief-laden sacrifice, and therefore the more precious? Was it because boys had to have all of the leisurely part of their lives packed into childhood before they became the workers and breadwinners? And in any case the psychological trick was superfluous, because, in spite of my jealousy, I shared everyone's adoration of him.

This began some little time after the visit to the surgery, when I went with my father to bring my mother and the baby home. We had a car at the time, I think because it belonged to my maternal grandfather, who was living with us. It must have been very old. In 1949 there were quite a few pre-war cars around that had been little used because of lack of petrol, but this car was on its last legs, if that can be said of a car. It had very large brass headlamps that stuck out, and saggy brown leather upholstery, the hot smell of which introduced me to travel sickness at a very early age.

The birth had taken place in Tynemouth, in what was called a nursing home, a house in a long, elegant grey terrace leading down towards the sea. It was early summer, but the sky was grey, meeting a darker grey sea over the cliff edge. I clambered from the car, feeling the immediate relief afforded by the wind-blown briny freshness of the air. A swoop of white birds mewed their alien cry above me, and I could see my mother standing in the window waiting for us. She was wearing a pink dress, and I somehow had the feeling that she had been there in that window, waiting ever since I had last seen her, which I then could not remember. I felt very, very sad.

Inside the house, my father disappeared into the room where my mother had been waiting. I wasn't allowed; for some reason I had germs. A nurse brought the baby out to me. She sat on the bottom step of the stairs, to bring him down to a level where I could see. Against the white shawl in which he was wrapped his skin looked cream; I was surprised by how tiny his face appeared. The nurse told me that he was the most beautiful baby in the house, and I was prepared to believe her, partly because as far as I could see he was the only one there, but also because I did find the fat smooth curve of his cheeks very pleasing. I felt something, and I didn't know what; a confusion, a sense of change and disorientation, and a desire for contact with him. I wanted to put my mouth to the little face, to nuzzle its softness and scent, to taste the newness of him. As I leaned forward, she stopped me. I could look but not touch, because of the germs.

At home, the presence of a new baby must have caused a bit of a squash. The house had three bedrooms, two modest doubles, occupied by our parents and the aforementioned grandfather, and a small single which was mine. Between our parents' bed and the window stood the big drop-side cot. After a while the space problem was solved because the grandfather died before the baby needed a room of his own.

I remember this grandfather with displeasure. His presence in the house during those first years of my life was at the centre of a feeling of anxiety and uncertainty, which I shared without understanding. To blame him was perhaps unjust. I suppose he was ill (he had heart problems), but he seemed to me to be merely bad-tempered and boring. He sat all day in an armchair beside the fire in the back room, listening to dance music on the radio but with no sign of enjoyment. His one pleasure in the day was at about five o'clock when he would have a glass of Guinness. Once or twice I was permitted to taste this, and I liked it, the biscuity bitterness lingering in the mouth, becoming milder and nuttier as it faded. Usually, however, I felt that he preferred to be unaware of me, even disliked my presence, and occasionally he frightened me. One afternoon, as the light faded into wintry darkness, I went into the room where he was sitting and struggled on tiptoe to touch the light switch, which was just within my reach. As the overhead light came on, his voice roared from behind me "Switch off that light". I jumped in fright, and one horrified glance over my shoulder showed him sitting in his usual chair, an oddly shaped bottle on the floor at his feet, and his trousers and pants around his ankles. Luckily my hand was still on the switch and with one leap I had the light off again and was out of the room.

The Guinness caused my mother a problem, as it meant she had to go to the off-licence on a regular basis. My parents were not teetotal, but they drank rarely, and certainly never had drink in the house, except at Christmas. I believe it was not just the Guinness, because one of the reasons for the visits to the off-licence involved the regular refilling of a large soda siphon. I loved the look of this, with the etched design in the glass, wire cage and elegantly curved handle and spout. But it was too heavy for me to lift even when empty. It was taken to the shop at the back of The Quarry Inn, at a time of day when my mother hoped she would not be seen to go in there, and brought back in a canvas shopping bag. This was strange because my grandfather had been a publican in his working life, and my mother had no embarrassment or shame about the fact that she had been brought up in a series of pubs and hotels.

By the time I was four years old, he had become more ill. During the dark winter evenings we would sit in the back room, the adults around the fire, myself at the dining table, drawing and colouring, or looking at picture books. Perhaps I would be on the floor playing with forgotten toys. Down there the air was cooler, and I was alert while the grown-ups dozed. The atmosphere was not cosy. There was a single overhead light, a bulb hanging within a clouded bowl suspended on chains. The room had space only for the dining furniture and the two armchairs, so my father usually sat on a dining chair, reading the paper. Such warmth as there was came from the small open fire, so that if you faced it, your front was warm and your back chilly. My mother would be knitting, the click of the needles and the rustle as the pages of the newspaper turned barely breaking the silence. Presumably the baby was sleeping in his cot upstairs.

Suddenly, a colder frisson in the atmosphere. Both parents pause in their slight activity, so that the shift and crackle of the fire sounds loudly into the silence. And a moment later, they are standing over the grandfather, patting a cheek, shaking a shoulder, running to the kitchen to return with water in a glass. He is not dead this time. Slowly he moves his grey head and face, his brow is wiped and a tartan rug tucked around his meagre body. My mother presumably realises that a child may be frightened by seeing her grandfather die in front of her, and reassuringly remarks, roughly in my direction, "He's only having a blackout". This has the form of a coherent sentence, so I assume that I have understood, but its meaning is obscured by the fact of a pile of black cotton sheets, with which I sometimes make a tent under the dining table. These, I know, are blackout curtains, which were used before I was born to keep the Germans away.

Still four years old, I went to stay for a few days with my Grandma, my father's mother, and a warm, benign presence in my life. She lived only a few miles away, where we visited frequently, so it was at that time unusual for me to stay with her overnight, although by the time I was six or seven I was doing so regularly. On my return, I found that the grandfather was not in the usual chair. Someone, assuming that I needed a comforting explanation, told me in a gentle voice that he had gone to be with Jesus. I felt uncertain about this, and cautiously looked for him behind every door.

The back bedroom became mine, for a while full of rather large and heavy furniture, relics of his last hotel home, and my brother moved from the cot into my small bedroom.

Then there is the other memory of that time when the grandfather was there, which exists as shreds and vestiges of feeling, interpreted through understanding imposed in adulthood on fears and impressions carried as from the earliest reaches of experience. Even now I do not know what happened, can guess only why a snatch of a tune heard distantly, why the idea of a certain kind of threat, still cause that atavistic recoil. It must be that the learning that a child does, during the stage of life where experience is so limited as to offer no explanation, remains unquestioned, unrecognised, unacknowledged, until later experience allows one to ask what it is that is being remembered. At a time when I did not have the language to give form to my fear, I learned unnamed emotions, and a sense that endurance gives a shell of self-reliance, the beginnings of my strange childhood in which it was difficult to be a child.

My bed was made with thin, yellowish woollen blankets in winter, instead of sheets. They were slightly scratchy, rather coarsely woven, with blanket-stitched hems sewn by hand in cream wool. More than fifty years later, I can still smell the odour of clean wet wool under my face, soaked by terrified tears and streaming mucus from my nose. I can feel again the harsh texture of the fabric, as I am held remorselessly face down, my skin scrubbed into the sweat-soaked wool under my body. As I scream and choke, something huge and horrible is forced into my bottom, my wrists are gripped, a weight settles onto the backs of my knees so that any movement is impossible. I am tiny, the force that holds me is beyond resistance, and most horribly of all, I learn, I learn, to restrain my screams, to control my struggles, because that way it will be over sooner, and we can pretend it did not happen.

Now in my mind is just that sense of powerlessness at the mercy of great strength, the physical memory of the weight and the pain, and the smell of the wet wool. And there was that dance music; it sounded like a theatre organ heard distantly, or the radio elsewhere in the house, cold music, not for pleasure, not made by people and instruments, but an accompaniment to a learning.

If that abuse did happen to me even before my true memories began at the age of three or four, who did it and how was it possible for it to occur? It was certainly not my father; no instinct even hints at that. Nor do I believe that it was the grandfather, although I feared him, his illness and his radio music.

Here are the little shreds of speculation that have a resonance of truth for me. Firstly, I know that if my father was at work, and my mother needed to go out, even just for shopping, someone had to come into the house to sit with the grandfather. For years after his death, there were friends and neighbours who were known for having performed that kindness. I wonder how often I accompanied her, or whether she took the opportunity to leave me at home and hurry out to complete the errands without the extra burden of a toddler in tow.

Secondly, throughout my childhood, I was afraid to be left with a babysitter, but never openly expressed that fear. Even after the death of the grandfather, our parents had a sparse social life, but when they did go out in the evening, Nell who ran the local sweet shop sat in the dining room stolidly knitting. My fear was not of her, but nevertheless I sat on the landing with my head resting on the banister until I heard my parents returning.

Thirdly, the helpers who sat with the grandfather tended to be men; perhaps this was his choice, perhaps my mother thought it more suitable. One of them was a distant relation of my father, not on the side of the family I came to know closely during my childhood. There must have been some babysitting involved too, although my parents hardly ever went out together in the evening, because I have a memory of sitting behind the upstairs banister watching the top of his head come in as those of my parents went out.

This man was at that time spoken of as being rather glamorous. He was a merchant seaman who travelled all over the world, and returned with gifts and stories from impossibly exotic places. For a while the presents that he brought back for me were memorably elaborate. One was a doll as tall as myself, with the ability to speak several sentences at the touch of a plastic diaphragm in its back, and which would walk beside me if I held its hand and swung its arm with a careful slow rhythm. This was a toy from America, a luxury beyond anything ordinary children would see in England in 1949, but I neither liked it nor wanted it. From time to time it would be brought out and I would be told how wonderful it was, and that I should be grateful. The idea of gratitude made me angry, and as soon as I could I put the doll away again in a cupboard at the back of the garage.

But strangely, the man disappeared and was not mentioned again, until years later, when I was fourteen or fifteen. No longer a sailor, he walked past our house each day on his way to the commuter train. I only knew who he was because I overheard the surprise and shock expressed between my parents the first time they saw him. The surprise to me was that they showed no inclination to speak to him, and when I remarked on this I was sharply forbidden to refer to him again. Something unmentionable had transformed him from the glamorous bringer of gifts, who trailed an aura of distant places, into someone to be avoided and shunned.

Lastly, from time to time when I was a young child, I would suffer a bit from constipation, which caused me to bleed copiously into the lavatory. I would show my mother the pan bright red with blood and she would tell me I had piles. Never did she take me to see any doctor about this, or allow me to mention it to anyone else. Yet she was the same mother who took me to the doctor when I was a teenager because my fingernails were rather inclined to break.

I believe my mother found out, and I believe that when something horrible happened to me, her father was in the house, listening to the distant dance music, the inhuman accompaniment to my screams or my silent agonised waiting for respite. She was above all an upholder of respectability; the activity was discovered and stopped, and for her the problem was solved by secrecy. What else could have been done for me anyway? The protection of family had been breached, and she attempted to shore it up without more disruption.

After this, my memories become whole, a continuous, almost seamless, stream of images reflecting a life which now seems to stretch back into history, although I am not yet old.

First School

The first class at Cullercoats Infants School was Miss Anderson's. No-one went to school before they were five years old in those days, or at least I did not know anyone who did so. As far as I was concerned it was soon enough. Although I quickly became adept and successful at the skills required in school, and enjoyed many of the activities, before long some of the demands became burdensome, and always I would have preferred not to be there.

As it was, I started a little late; perhaps I had been ill again. On my first day, my mother took me into the school, and all the other children were already there inside the classroom; I had the impression they had been there already for several days. Miss Anderson took my mother into the room, leaving me outside in the corridor. The door handle was just at nose height, and I stood and looked at it fixedly while my mother and my teacher exchanged information, presumably about me. The handle was shiny brass, a curved art nouveau style with a thumb-catch. I could see the reflection of my face in the half cylinder of handle, strangely elongated. As I rocked backwards and forwards, first the top of my head, then my chin, stretched out amusingly. I experimented with different faces; fat cheeks puffed out, open mouth, protruding tongue. Fortunately, by the time the door opened again, I was bored by this and leaned my back against the wall at the side of the door in order to admire my new brown Start-rite shoes.

Then, my mother was gone, and I was in the classroom, shown to my place, given something to do. I was not nervous; several of the children were already known to me, and I was aware that in other parts of the school were the big girls from our street who would find me and look after me at play-time, and when it was time to go home. I set my mind to doing the tasks I was given and generally enjoyed them.

The school building dated from about 1880, a sturdy brick block, single storey but with high ceilings. The windows were tall, flooding the rooms with light, but the sills were above a child's head height, so it was impossible to look out. A deliberate design feature on the part of the Victorian architects, who considerately reduced the opportunity to daydream and be distracted from the lesson. At each end of the building was a concrete yard, one for boys and one for girls, and this segregation was exercised at this time, although it was relaxed later. The principal reason for the division was that at the back of each yard, behind a tall brick wall were the toilets, a row of icy cubicles each containing a big white pan with a cold wooden seat and a long pull chain. This was on the girls' side; I believe the boys had a rather more primitive drain to use, and one cubicle into which they put small new boys and held the door shut. Another feature of the yard was that if it rained we all huddled into an open-fronted 'dutch barn' shelter against one wall. It was cold at home but it was even colder at school.

We were all only five years old, but we sat at double desks, facing towards the teacher and the blackboard. The desks had a black cast-iron frame, a long wooden seat and lift-up lids beneath which we kept our necessary equipment. At first this was minimal. We did not even have writing materials. It amuses me a little nowadays that little children in nursery and infants' class 'play' with sand and water, on the understanding that this play introduces a number of skills of dexterity and even begins the process of learning aspects of science. We also used sand, but in our case it was the initial step in the process of learning to write. A shallow tray contained a thin layer of sand, and in this we practised forming the shapes of the letters with a forefinger. Only when Miss Anderson was satisfied that all the lower case letters could be recognised and traced in the sand did a pupil move on to the next stage. Still there was no paper or pencil; we used little wood-framed blackboards and a stick of white chalk. This board had a series of parallel lines marked on it, so that the letters could be formed between them. Short letters (a c e m etc.) were one line high, tall ones (b d h and so on) were two lines tall, and the ones with dangling tails stretched down a line. This appealed to my sense of order, the co-ordination of finger and eye came easily, and I began on a school career in which my successes were to be both pleasurable and burdensome.

My nature was to be obedient and compliant, and I learned quickly and easily. I had a retentive memory, which suited the way children were taught in those days. I can still feel the rhythm of reciting 'one and one are two, two and two are four, three and three are six'. It irritated me when we got to 'seven and seven are fourteen', not because it became difficult to remember, but because the rhythm was broken. It would have been possible to keep up the pace, but some children started to lag after that, and I couldn't understand why they did not try to maintain the pattern of the chant.

Of course, there were other, less-regimented, activities, also enjoyable. I cannot actually remember painting in the first Infants class, but I do remember clay, orangey-brown, slimy and cold. It could be squidged out between the fingers, rolled into sausages and balls, and squeezed onto the end of a thumb to make doll-size cups. In order to keep it workable, it had to be mashed up with water from time to time, then smacked repeatedly onto a stained wooden board to get it back into shape. This reminded me of the mud pies I made in the garden at home. Mud pies were a kind of traditional thing associated with childhood, and 'imaginative', otherwise the mess would have rendered them unacceptable to my mother.

Another activity that took place outside of the classroom was Music and Movement. I hated this. It was a radio programme, in which worthy music and a prissy voice accompanied attempts to contort one's body in various ways. 'Crouch down as small as you can' and 'stretch up tall' were silly and pointless enough, but 'be a tree' was excruciating. After a few of these programmes I realised that the activity was almost bearable if you followed the instructions as minimally as was possible without getting shouted at by the teacher, but I never could see the purpose of it.

It wasn't that I was against sport or exercise. We had another lesson out in the school yard in which we ran little races, chased wooden hoops, threw beanbags and jumped over ropes. I enjoyed all of that. Nor was it that I was without imagination or a liking for drama. The favourite game in the playground involved acting out complex stories based on fairy-tale personalities and situations. The principal character was Prince Hal, there was a beautiful princess whose name I forget, and the plot always included escapes from dragons, hiding in magic castles and galloping about on imaginary horses.

This liking for adventurous and romantic stories was almost an obsession in my imagination and private inner life at the time. It always took me a long time to get to sleep at night, and I used this time to make up stories about myself, and other interesting characters of my acquaintance. My Sunday school teacher, Miss Fish, had a great deal of curly blonde hair, which made her in my view a story princess. I knew she was engaged to be married, so I invented an elaborate wedding ceremony for her. It was entirely fictional, as I had never been to a wedding, and had only the vaguest notion of what it entailed, other than beautiful dresses.

More importantly, I was in love myself, and this gave me an opportunity to indulge in a whole series of fantasies in which the object of my affection satisfied my desires. The feeling I experienced was intense; remembering it is the most potent reminder to me about what it is to be a little child. It is as serious, as significant, as dignified as any stage of adulthood. Inside the head and heart of every child is a self-awareness as strong as yours, or mine as I experience it now. I loved Miss Snowdon, the teacher at school who played the piano. I don't think she ever even spoke to me, but I adored the movement of her hands as she played. She looked slightly sad to me, as though burdened by some secret tragedy, and I dreamed of how her discovery of my love for her would make her happy. On her left index finger she wore a gold signet ring, and one day, in a conversation with a friend quite unrelated to any of my preoccupations, my mother provided me with the information that wearing a ring on that finger meant a woman was advertising her availability for love. I was entranced that such a message could be conveyed so easily to those who chose to notice it. Above all, Miss Snowdon had a large, softly rounded bosom, unlike any woman in my family, and I was fascinated with how this would feel. In my night-time story-telling to myself, my favourite fiction was one in which I had fallen in the school playground and cut my knee. She was the only teacher around, so although she did not actually know me, inevitably she had to take care of me. First of all, she knelt at my feet, tending to the wound, then she looked up into my eyes, saw there whatever was needed to cement our relationship, and took me in her arms. I felt myself held on her lap, curled against the soft bosom, in supreme and ecstatic comfort. Strangely, I have no memory at all of sitting in any person's lap in reality, although my family was not particularly unaffectionate.

After Miss Anderson, I moved into the top Infants' class, that of Mrs. Douglas. This move was more than usually complex for us, as we also moved into a new school building. It was 1951, and the first phase of moving out of the old Victorian edifice into a brand new modern building near to the sea front on Mast Lane, which would eventually become the Cullercoats Primary School. For us, the first batch, the change lasted only one year, because as Juniors we would return to the old building in John Street. On the moving day, we emptied the contents of our desks into brown cardboard boxes of a size that we could carry, then walked the half mile or so to the new building two by two in a talkative but orderly line.

What a contrast in our surroundings! The new school had large windows looking out over a wide area of grass, and a single vast expanse of playground to be shared by boys and girls. There were toilets indoors, with wash basins, and there were toys. During wet playtimes, we could play in the hall, where there was a huge and terrifying rocking horse, with a flowing white mane and red wooden rockers which could have crushed the feet of any child incautious enough to stand too close.

However, although school had this superficially more leisurely aspect, by now I was fulfilling a role for my parents, principally my mother, that was at once exciting, gratifying and horribly burdensome. I was the Cleverest Child, and I do not mean in the family; I mean, if not in the world, certainly in my mother's circle of acquaintance. Later, I came to realise she needed me to shore up her self image as the mother of some type of unassailable example to other people's children. Luckily, it was easy for me to meet the criteria. In a sense I was inventing them, as my parents reacted to my achievements rather than specifying them. At the age of six, I could read fluently, even the editorial column of the News Chronicle, which my father presented to me each evening. I did not understand it, of course, but I could look at and say the words. My own story books I read voraciously; I remember noticing at about that age that I had developed rough callused elbows because I spend so much time lying on my stomach leaning on them as I read. Numbers were readily understood at that level too, as they were logical, patterned and could be learned by recitation, which was another of my skills. Actually, I think my parents probably started the process of giving me Cleverest Child status way before school; another early memory is of being able to recite most of Jim Who Was Eaten By A Lion standing on their bed when my brother was still occupying the cot.

Admiration and status were all very well, however. The burden of expectation struck me in a way I could not have anticipated during that year as a Top Infant. I was given a very responsible job, that of Chief Milk Monitor. This was because I was the only child in the class who could reliably tell the time. My function was to watch out for it to be twenty minutes past ten in the morning, whereupon I would remind Mrs. Douglas that the team of five or six milk monitors had to go to the school hall to prepare the milk for playtime. In the hall were several metal crates containing the small bottles (each of one third of a pint) of free milk which was kindly provided for all children by the government. The monitors took out the bottles from the crates, lined them up on a long counter-top, took off the cardboard tops and stuck a waxed paper straw in each one. By the time this was done, the rest of the children started to file through in order to collect their drinks. The importance of my role was emphasised to me, not only by Mrs. Douglas, who had chosen me, but also by the head teacher, Mrs. Huntley. The whole of the morning timetable hinged on my ability to have everything ready for playtime to begin. I was proud, but also confident that it was easy for me to perform a task which I knew to be within my capabilities. The attitude of my parents I now know to have been unfortunate, to say the least. They gave me to understand that, yes, they were proud of my status, but that it was only to be expected that the Cleverest Child would find herself in such a position.

One morning, not long before I was to give the customary signal for the monitors to be on the move, the classroom door opened and in came Mrs. Huntley. She was a stout lady with sandy hair tied rather severely back from her very round face. I used to think that she was plump because she must be associated with Huntley and Palmer's Biscuits and had clearly over-indulged. Mrs. Douglas seemed surprised to see her; it was unusual for her to appear in the classroom. With no preamble that I can recall, she announced to Mrs. Douglas and the class that she had decided that we should have a change of milk monitors. She then read out a list of names. Every one of them was a member of the existing team, but my name was missing. I had been sacked, without warning or explanation.

As the team left the room, I could see that they too were puzzled and perhaps shocked. I felt physically sick with mortification. In my ears I suddenly felt gushing waves of pulse, and burning tears bathed my eyes like hot acid. Trying to hide this visible reaction to my downfall, I lifted the lid of my desk, and desperately pretended to be tidying the contents. In the moment before hiding my face I had seen pity in the eyes of Mrs. Douglas, and she quickly and briskly distracted the class with a pressing task.

Whether or not that was the end of the matter in school, I don't recall. Certainly, the incident was never explained to me, and I never could think of any misdeed that would have justified it. If only I could have gone home to my mother and wept. If only I could have railed against the unfairness, expressed my bitter hatred of the fat woman who had come into the room and so casually humiliated me. If only I could have been comforted, cuddled, assured that it was of no importance, that I was still valued, loved and important. This did not happen, however. Already, at the age of six, I knew that my mother would be ashamed, that she would be in some way diminished by my failure. I felt the terrible burden of responsibility, knowing that my mother *needed* me to be the Cleverest Child, and that I had to uphold this in order to safeguard something in her. So I said nothing, and held the pain silently within me until school life moved on and I had other achievements to offer.

My Grandma

My grandmother, born Alice Watson in 1883, was the second of four siblings, all of whom survived into old age. This was perhaps unusual for the time, but for this family poverty was not an issue; a photograph I have of them shows a respectable, well-nourished and smartly dressed group.

The photograph must have been taken in about 1890; my grandmother appears to be six or seven years old. Her elder brother Frederick, a handsome sturdy boy with bright blonde hair, wearing a smart cutaway jacket, stands in front of their father. My grandmother, Alice, and her younger sister, Elizabeth, are wearing identical plaid frocks with large white lace collars and cuffs, and the baby, Sarah, staring suspiciously at the camera from their mother's lap, is in white with a plaid sash. Alice holds a little basket and Elizabeth clutches a posy. My great-grandmother, Ann, and great-grandfather, James, are a very good-looking couple. She, in her black high-necked dress, has a solemn round face with large dark eyes and dark hair parted centrally and sleeked severely back, except for what appears to be one curling tendril escaping behind her left ear. He, in his suit and soft bow tie, is elegantly bearded, with regular features and a long straight nose. They are the epitome of the middle class Victorian family.

I see, in this photograph, how fearfully rapid is the passage of time. In words, nineteenth and twenty-first, two centuries separate my grandmother and me. Here am I, with perhaps a quarter of my life still to live, looking at this girl, already a young woman when Queen Victoria died. I feel no links between my own life and the time during which my own parents grew up and formed their values, in the early part of the twentieth century, but this Victorian child passed to me an enormous legacy of attitude about behaviour, manners, consideration and family affection, none of which has proved false.

I first became aware of my Grandma as a member of a strange and unorthodox household during the time that it was being set up. My great uncle, William Davidson, known as Uncle Willy, had a spacious house built in 1947 on the edge of North Shields away from the river. It stood near the top of the long gradual incline from the town towards the countryside on the road to Newcastle, and he called it The Crest. Here, whether through philanthropy, a strong sense of family loyalty, or the selfishness of a man who liked to be looked after, he was to accommodate a group, which in retrospect I can see was rather odd, but which for many years I simply took for granted. Uncle Willy was the husband of Elizabeth (or Aunt Lizzie), the middle girl in the photograph. In the family, there was always a sense that he had conferred favours and generosity, for which there should be gratitude and repayment, of an emotional nature. My little brother bore some of this in the form of having been named after Uncle Willy and Aunt Lizzie's only child, a boy who had tragically died of diphtheria at the age of fifteen, in about 1920. They had attempted the survival of a family surname that was about to die out by naming the boy Kirton. My mother, in a moment of sentiment when she was engaged to my father, said that if ever she had a son she would give him that name in memory of the lost one. They did not forget. When my brother was old enough to choose a name for himself, and was tired of jokes about how drawn he looked, he called himself Kit, and everyone except Aunt Lizzie followed suit.

Uncle Willy and Aunt Lizzie had in some slightly disreputable way, involving the lending of money, become rich. This gave them a discernible self-importance. One sign of this was in the organisation of their unusual household, as a result of which they never performed any household tasks.

Next in status to Uncle Willy and Aunt Lizzie was Grandma. She had been widowed in 1935, and had since then been living in Howdon on Tyne, with her only son, my father, then alone after he married in 1942. She, I now realise, worked as the housekeeper at The Crest, mostly responsible for shopping and cooking.

Also in the house was great-uncle Fred, the handsome, confident boy of the old photograph. Until he became too old, or tired, or ill, to work at all, which happened quite early in my childhood, he performed the heavier tasks of gardening, looking after the fires and doing the odd household repair. His wife, Rebecca, had died young and childless, leaving him helpless in the way that men were allowed to be in those days. Also, a widower was an unusual creature in those days after a world war, and around him always hung the feeling that if his sisters had not been there to protect him he would have been the prey of rapacious widows.

Next in line of importance was a very old lady, Mrs. Crow. She, also long widowed and childless, had been Grandma's next-door neighbour in Howdon, and as she would have been too lonely when Grandma moved to The Crest, it was decided that she should come too. She was general assistant in the kitchen department. Except on Boxing Day when the whole lot of them went to visit the other sister, Sarah, who lived less than half a mile away, I cannot remember Mrs. Crow ever leaving the house. She had suffered from rickets in childhood, and had the characteristic bowed legs and rolling gait. We children called her Auntie Crow, although we were vaguely aware that her name was Margaret, but we knew she was not really family. This was confirmed by the fact that, although she and my grandmother were the closest of friends, they always called each other Mrs. Crow and Mrs. Hull.

Last of all was Bella. She lived somewhere else, down near the Fish Quay, and may have had some family of her own, never mentioned except by implication; Grandma would give her a loaf or a cake or a pie to take home on baking days, much too large for her to consume alone. Aunt Lizzie called Bella 'the servant', but everyone else called her Bella. She had false teeth that were excessively even and white, and set in bright orange gums, and her arms to above the elbows were red and shiny, like the leather chairs in the sitting room. Her jobs were cleaning and washing, which she did every weekday. She had weekends off, but came in on Christmas Day to do the washing up after my Grandma and Mrs. Crow had prepared dinner for up to twenty.

So, three of the four children in the photograph lived together in that house for the first few years of my childhood, and the fourth was just around the corner. I loved my Grandma the best, but the household as a whole was warm, and busy, and full of interest. My parents, my brother and I went there for tea every Sunday, but as soon as I was old enough, I began to spend as much time as I could staying with this strange collection of elderly relations and their appendages. They took an interest in my progress and achievements at school and elsewhere, but not a jot of their affection depended on my continued success. I knew instinctively that to my Grandma I would continue to be one of the two most loveable children in the world even had I been like Joyce Tweddle, who sniffed and slightly wet herself in the corner of our classroom, as she made little sandcastles from the writing material.

Our most important qualification for being loved was that we were the children of our father, or as Grandma described us 'Our James's Bairns'. This was an immutable role, requiring no work on our part, or, more specifically, on my part. I don't believe Kit ever felt any obligation to be anything other than his natural self. The security of having been born into that circle of affection that centred on our father was luxurious to me. I did not have to achieve anything, or be anything, or represent anything, that was not automatically mine through my Grandma's much-loved son. I was very happy to be one of The Bairns.

Sleeping in the house was not the most comfortable experience. Because the usual inhabitants used up all the bedrooms, I had to sleep with Grandma in her big bed. There was a little single bar electric fire in the room, a very modern innovation, I should say, but central heating was out of the question for domestic purposes, so the room was cold. The bed was high and had a horse-hair mattress which was hard, no other word for it. Often I would watch Bella starching and ironing the white linen sheets, so I knew why they lay as stiff as boards across the bed, leaving a wide passage for cold air down each side of my winceyetted body. At the bottom of the bed were two hot water bottles, big round things made of pot, which at night were too hot to put your feet on, and in the morning lay there like ice blocks, ready to wake you with a start if you accidentally came in contact with them. It was really difficult to get to sleep.

After a while Grandma would come to bed. I knew it was impolite to watch her undress, but I was fascinated by the various layers she disclosed, so I made a pretence of sleep and lay still while she disrobed. First would go the pinafore she wore over her clothes. This was actually like a sleeveless dress, made of flowered cotton. Under it were her respectable lady's clothes, probably a tweed skirt and a hand-knitted twinset in muted colours. Sometimes, if it was particularly cold winter weather, she would wear a very finely knit long sleeved garment called a spencer beneath the twin set. Then there was a peach sateen petticoat, a pretty colour, but not glamorous with its vest shaped top. Off came knee length bloomers, usually pink, then the corset, a formidable garment which covered from the arm-pits to top of thigh, with bone stiffeners and a long row of silvery hooks and eyes down the front.

Suspenders on the bottom edge of the corset held up sturdy beige stockings. Because she suffered from what she called dropped arches and hammer toes, she wore under the stockings various appliances of elastic around her feet, and these came off next. Finally there was the long fine woollen vest. What was under that lot I never knew because the vest stayed on underneath a beautiful ankle-length broderie anglais nightdress. Out came a double set of false teeth which went into a glass at the side of the bed. The last of the preparations was the pink hairnet, which served to keep her wavy white hair neat from day to day. Clean vest and bloomers were put out for the morning, but I never saw the dressing process, as my late night and the fact that she was up and working shortly after six o'clock meant that I slept through it.

Once she was in bed I could start to warm up and feel sleepy. I would slide over the glossy stiff sheet into the warmth of her back, or she would say, 'Ooh you're chilly,' and cuddle me up until I felt cosy and comfortable. It was advisable to get to sleep first, because if she beat me to it, her snoring would resonate around the room. For such a gentle and soothing person, asleep she could rival a lion for roars. Somehow I didn't mind, and once she had settled into a rhythm I allowed the sound to synchronise with my own breathing.

One remaining problem of Grandma's bedroom could arise with the need to go to the toilet (or, as we called it, the lav), as it was along a dark corridor and downstairs. Actually, no-one used the bathroom in the night. There was a pot under every bed, and the first job each morning for Bella was to empty and wash them. The two from upstairs, ours and Uncle Fred's, were put on the bottom stair, each with a cloth over it to hide the contents. I never thought there was anything odd about this, although in my own home there was no question but that you went to the lavatory in the night if necessary. I suppose I thought it was because they were all too old to be able to walk from their bedrooms.

Another memorable thing about Grandma's bedroom was a magnificent Victorian tallboy, which stood against one wall. It was glossy polished wood the colour of conkers, with round black knobs on the drawers. Almost the height of the room, it contained piles of interesting clean undergarments, bedlinen, hats and furs. The white cotton embroidered nightdresses lay in neatly pressed piles, alongside finely stitched cotton quilts. These she told me she had made herself in preparation for her marriage; as she expressed it, for her 'bottom drawer'. This concerned me a little, as it was clear that this process had started well before any marriage was planned, or even before the potential husband had been met. This was obvious, as it must have taken an age to make each of these exquisite items. I wondered whether I should be making a start on my own. This seemed to be tempting fate, as my mother would from time to time remind me that with her looks to inherit, I should not make any assumptions about growing up beautiful, and should prepare to look after myself by working hard at school.

In a top drawer of the dresser, irritatingly out of reach, was an old biscuit tin in which Grandma kept chocolate; Fry's Chocolate Cream, or Five Boys, and tubes of Wine Gums, which would be given out only on Sundays before we went home. Then one day, I found in one drawer a carefully folded pillowcase, containing a stiffly laundered large sheet, another of the lovely night dresses and two bright shiny pennies. When I asked why these things were there, Grandma casually told me they were for laying her out when she was dead; the pennies were to put on her eyes. The idea of her being dead seemed so remote, I thought it excessively cautious of her to have made these preparations already. But I liked the bright pennies and the crisp whiteness of the linen.

Our Sunday visits were a ritual part of childhood family life, and almost entirely enjoyable. My parents, my brother and I had midday dinner at home then set off for The Crest, where we would have tea. We did not have a car, and the journey required two buses. The first took us past Tynemouth, into North Shields, where we walked into Northumberland Square to await the next bus. The square was elegant with its grey stone terraces of early Victorian, perhaps even Georgian, houses. It was fun, because its grassy centre was intersected by paths bordered with low stone walls along which my brother and I could balance and run. It was educational, because the walls had rows of metal stubs in them, which my father explained as the remains of smart railings, taken away to be melted down and made into bullets during the recent war. If we had more than a few minutes to wait for the bus, we were allowed to run down a side street to look at the Wooden Dolly, the almost unrecognisably weathered remains of a life-sized carved figure of a fishwife in her long skirt, with her creel (the covered basket that held the fish) on her back.

Soon the red double-decker bus would come; I found the second half of the journey much more interesting. We passed the Infirmary, where according to my mother people only went in order to die, and I imagined the horror of finding yourself unexpectedly turning in at the gates, suddenly realising what was in store for you. Then there was Tynemouth High School, where my father had been a pupil more than thirty years before, an ideal schoolboy, who had been captain of football and cricket, very clever but forced to leave and earn money because he had the opportunity of a secure job in spite of The Depression. This word 'depression' I knew as an illness acknowledged only in rather disapproving whispers, so I didn't quite understand why his education had been curtailed. Then there was the car showroom, where, for what seems years in my memory, stood an Armstrong Siddeley Sapphire Saloon, an object of unattainable desire for my father. Cars were actually quite sparse on the roads at that time. When we waited at our bus stop, only five or six may pass. If one of them contained someone of our acquaintance, my father, a gentlemanly and mild-mannered man, would quietly intone, 'Bloated plutocrats'. He had a love of words.

One day on the bus a very strange thing happened. I was seven years old, in class 1A of the Juniors, and my teacher was Miss Howey. There she sat, facing us on the long plush seat that ran along the side of the bus at the rear. Her plain rather flat face was topped as usual by her carefully waved dull brown hair. She was wearing her customary brown suit, a tailored jacket and pleated skirt, with thick beige stockings and brown laced shoes held neatly together. All absolutely as normal, except that at her side sat another Miss Howey, in every detail precisely the same.

Once at Grandma's, the afternoon followed a predictable but comforting routine. I had my scrapbooks to work on. There were two of these. One contained pictures of the Royal Family, taken by Grandma from the newspapers during the week, then carefully stuck onto the pages of grey sugar paper by me. There were the two princesses Elizabeth and Margaret, dressed rather like the Misses Howey, and looking to me almost as old as their parents. King George, shaking hands with dignitaries, and the Queen, smiling with her teeth gritted, were the objects of a distant ambition. Every lesson of politeness and table manners instilled into me were to be taken seriously, so that, if one ever found one's self in the presence of the Queen, one would know how to behave. This was, of course, the same kind of worst-or-best-case scenario as always wearing clean knickers in case of being run over by a bus. Nevertheless, how proud my Grandma would have been had she known that in December 2000 all the preparations came to fruition. Different Queen of course, but same manners.

The second scrap book was a genuine relic of Victorian pastimes. It was possible still at that time to buy paper scraps, most of which were cut-out details from great works of art. I loved the shiny slightly embossed texture of them, and willingly spent an hour arranging them to best effect on the page then gluing the backs with Cow Gum on a stumpy brush. My favourite was the pair of Botticelli putti which must have been in

Shakespeare's mind when he had Romeo mention 'the white upturned wondering eyes'. It is easy to speculate on the pointlessness of the lives that held it permissible to spend time sticking printed coloured pictures into books, but in fact I, like many a Victorian young lady long before me, learned a considerable familiarity with the Old Masters from them.

Teatime was a demonstration of Grandma's baking skills. Some of my favourites were a lusciously juicy bilberry tart with extra castor sugar sprinkled over it, sponge cake with big hot pieces of crystallised ginger in it, sticky treacly gingerbread on which we spread chunks of butter, egg and cress sandwiches filled so thickly the contents fell on the plate with a plop when you attempted to bite them, and a wonderful savoury pie of egg custard and pieces of ham, with a pastry lid. When it was your birthday, there were buttered scones, in one of which a folded scrap of greaseproof paper held a silver threepenny piece, the plate carefully positioned so that the birthday person picked up the special scone. Always, the table was meticulously set, with the white lace of paper doilies under the cakes and tarts. In the centre of the table, the most elaborate cake stood high in a moulded glass stand. The impossibly delicate china was white with turquoise leaves and flowers and gold rims, and each of us had a large white damask napkin, ironed to cardboard stiffness, to spread on our laps.

I cannot remember when the television appeared at The Crest; it was at a time when there was only one channel, and that was the BBC, and years before we had one at home in Newton Avenue. Uncle Willy liked modern technology although he clung to the past too. In the kitchen of his house, brand new in 1948, was a built-in range, the same as any Victorian one except that it was yellowish enamel and did not need blacking. The gas stove in the scullery did most of the cooking, however. Apart from warming our night-clothes, the range seemed only to be used at Christmas, when its oven slowly roasted one of two or three geese needed for our massive dinner.

Another of Uncle Willy's other notable forays into the use of modern gadgets had been in the 1920s when he bought a pressure cooker and sued the shop. He somehow ended up in court demanding his money back because the cooker did not make gravy to his liking.

Some time early in the 1930s he had bought a car. Of course at that time there was no such thing as the driving test, and the purchaser simply drove away from the showroom after a brief explanation as to which pedals were which. Uncle Willy had the sense to take with him my father, who was already a competent driver, but insisted on doing the driving himself. Suddenly, to my father's alarm, Uncle Willy began to fling the steering wheel from side to side, causing the car to veer wildly. When he could be persuaded to stop, my father breathlessly asked him just what he thought he was doing.

'Whey, lad,' said Uncle Willy, 'yon's a brend new car. Ye divvent want us to gan through the puddles and get it aal clarty d'ye?'

Anyway, the television put a stop to scrap books; in one day of 1953 or '54 we moved from the amusements of the 19th century to those of the 20th. Before tea we watched Sooty followed by The Brains Trust. Without meaning in any way to sound intellectually pretentious, even at the age of seven I preferred The Brains Trust. I can't remember the topics discussed, but the names bring back to me the feeling that pervaded the sitting room on those Sunday afternoons, my father in particular engrossed by the privilege of listening to A.J.Ayer, Marganhita Laski, Aldous Huxley, Dr. Bronowski, Lord Harewood.

Although those Sunday afternoons of childhood provided the comfortable, reliable warmth of affection, the best times were those I spent on outings with Grandma. Some were simple. In North Shields there was a small department store, Hill Carter's, that had a restaurant with wide windows looking out over the river. Here we would have cups of tea and hot buttered teacakes, watching the activity on the water. At that time Port of Tyne was very busy, so there would usually be a huge cargo ship sliding slowly up-river surrounded by bustling tugs with slapping white bow waves. Smaller craft, including fishing vessels bobbing in and out of the Fish Quay, would dodge each other over the spreading grey wake of the ship. We could see the slow dance of the cranes moving over the shipyards, while around and above them swooped and dived the crying silver gulls.

For me, there was a sense of linking with cold places. The black and white passenger liners, Venus and Leda, would start their stately journey out into the North Sea towards Norway, the place where Vikings had come from so long ago. The rust red trawlers battering their way out into the heavy seas were heading for Iceland to find cod, and sometimes there would be a story of one which had foundered under the weight of ice which built up in sheets over its superstructure, so that the boat turned turtle under its weight.

My favourite vessel of all was the ferry, which ran across between North Shields and South Shields. From time to time Grandma and I made the ten-minute trip across river, either to go to the market in South Shields, or just to turn round and come back again. I don't know when the boat was built, but it was a perfect little steam vessel, which carried about fifty passengers and two or three cars. As it rose and fell at its jetty a wide ramp ground slowly down, while I skipped about, impatient to be allowed to go on board. We needed to climb quickly to the upper deck in order to sit on the slatted seats of varnished wood, which covered boxes full of lifebelts, there ready to save us if the boat sank, I was told. So there was an exciting element of danger. On the way up we peeped into the engine room to smell the heat and the steam, and to see the great turning and pumping and gasping machinery of shining brass. A breathy whistle from up by the single tall funnel announced our departure, and we turned round into the bustle and flurry of the sea-lane. Sometimes a great ship would be bearing down towards us, or smaller vessels heeled round our sides as we ploughed across their path. The air smelled of fish and steam and the sea, and sometimes of the fertiliser factory on the South Shields bank of the river, the Guano Works. Had I known that guano was seabirds' droppings mined on islands in an ocean on the other side of the world, where it lay thicker than the height of a man, I could have seen some glamour in it. As it was, it was just a bad smell.

The river and the sea were a familiar part of life to Grandma. Her husband, long dead before I was born, and known to me only as a handsome photograph on her dressing table, had been a seagoing engineer in the Merchant Service. A young widower when he met and married her, he said that he was not going to spend his life away from this wife, so he left the sea and took passage on the river instead. The Tyne Commissioner, the civil servant who supervised the running of the port, had a steam yacht, which acted as his office, and my grandfather became its master. However, Grandma's links with the land were just as strong as those with the sea, as her mother's family were farmers south of the river. This gave us the opportunity for another regular outing, to Dene Farm, a bus ride out of Consett, in the gentle rolling countryside of County Durham.

The farm was run by Jack, who was, I believe, the son of my Grandma's cousin. He had a wife, whose name I have forgotten, and three daughters, Audrey, Vera and Mary. I can remember little of these girls, all of whom were older than I, but I have a number of strong pictorial memories of the farm. We got off the bus at the top of a long sloping lane, bordered by trees, under which we once found wild strawberries, mouth-achingly sweet with flavour. At the end of the lane, the house stood by a wide stony yard, at one edge of which was a round metal water trough for the cattle. Sometimes I sailed a clockwork boat on this, until one day it sank.

Of the house I remember only one room, which seemed to comprise the whole of the ground floor. This had a large open fire at one end, surrounded by the kind of leather-topped fender you can sit on. Along one side of the room was a large table, with perhaps a dozen chairs around it. The floor was, I think, stone slabs. Stairs led up from one corner, but I was never allowed to go up there. Outside was a privy, a brick shed housing a single plank seat with a round hole cut in it. Your business fell through, not very far, and got shovelled out into a midden surrounded by a high fence of corrugated iron. I had feelings of shuddering horror about this, not least because it stank, but also because I knew that the contents, when rotted down, got taken away to be spread on the vegetable garden, and often one would be expected to eat vegetables here. Worst of all was the work that went into its management. I knew that one of the men who worked on the farm had to do this shovelling, and I dreaded adulthood if it meant work in which there was this degree of subservience. To be in no position to refuse when told to go into this mess of stinking slurry seemed to me to be worse than what I had been told of slavery in sunny cotton fields.

Other memories are much more pleasant. Eggs had to be collected from wherever they had been laid. The intense satisfaction of pushing aside the grass under the hedge and finding two warm white eggs, or turning over the straw in the barn and filling a basket! It was a bit haphazard, but after a while we could not find any more, so the job was done.

The barn beside the house was high, and open down one side. At each end was a great loose pile of hay or straw, and from the middle hung a swing. Its arc was wide and slow because the ropes were so long, and the big brave girls swung high, then jumped off into the hay. I never felt able to do this, so I swung and swung, until I felt seasick and had to sit on a little chair by the fire, sipping cold milk while everyone else ate their dinner.

Milking was still partly done by hand. I suppose the milk production was the main function of the farm, as I remember several cows standing in a row attached to the rhythmical shushing of a machine, but milk for the kitchen was extracted by hand into a white enamel bowl. Several times I was offered a lesson in how to do this, but as I knew for a fact that a cow was capable of kicking forwards with its back legs, I declined. It was interesting enough to watch the squeeze and pull, and to hear the ping of the jet as it hit the metal.

I don't remember sheep, although there may have been some, as there were definitely two sheep dogs, black and white collies called Glen and Lassie. It never surprised me that the clever dog on the television that I saw a year or two later was called Lassie, since that was plainly the correct name for that kind of dog, and had it been male it would have been called Glen. Glen at the farm was a dangerous challenge, as he was Not A Pet, and therefore not to be touched. If approached he would trot away with a sidelong look over his shoulder, and if you persisted would suddenly turn on you with a blood-curdling snarl. Needless to say, I tried this experiment but once. Lassie was more amenable to company, and when not at work would amble around beside us, sniffing for eggs.

At busy times, hay-making and harvest, the farm seemed to fill up with men, I suppose semi-itinerant workers, or groups from neighbouring farms who helped each other out. Everyone, including Grandma, had a job in the fields. The harvest had not changed much over a few hundred years. Although there was machinery, driven by a steam engine, my memory is of the men cutting rhythmically with scythes, and the women making stooks, where tall bundles of corn were stood together to make a sort of wigwam. By the time I was nine or ten I was big enough to learn how to use the long-tined fork, to help with the pitching of hay into great piles on a horse drawn cart. At midday, the children, including myself, carried baskets of bread, cold sausages and cheese, and jugs of tea into the field, and threw hay around until shouted at that we had destroyed the morning's work. The scent of the hay, the quiet voices and the stamp and jingle of the horse were the harmony of summer.

Later in the day, a meal was served at the big table indoors. I would like to describe tucking into hearty old-fashioned farmhouse fare, but all I can remember is a mutton stew with lumps of gristle so impenetrable that the feeling of the half-chewed fat in my throat threatened vomiting. So I slid off my chair and crawled around on the floor amongst a variety of boots and the odour of damp corduroys.

Another very different regular treat given to me by my Grandma was the pantomime. She and I went together every year on or near my birthday at the end of November, to buy our tickets. Those little stiff cards, with the words Mother Goose, or Alladin, or Cinderella, were placed carefully into a zipped pocket of her purse, while I skipped around her in an ecstasy of anticipation. Always we went in January or February, so the dead grey time after Christmas was over held that promise of the treat to come.

The Theatre Royal in Newcastle seemed to me a place of magic. Behind its great portico of grey stone columns we entered a foyer of dark red plush carpets, ceilings painted with the angels and cherubs of my scrap book, glittering gilt mirrors, broad staircases with gleaming brass handrails which, to me, could have been solid gold. In the auditorium we sat below rows of glittering lights, among the excited cacophony of voices as the audience gathered. It was an occasion for dressing up, and I remember a full-skirted, dark blue taffeta dress, with marcasite buttons on the front that sparkled like clusters of ice chips. The fabric rustled luxuriously as I settled into my velvet chair, the seat of which rocked precariously, as I was too short to get my feet to the floor.

For me, the most exciting moment was when the unseen orchestra in the pit began to tune up. The random discords and harmonies that heralded the opening scene gradually signalled a spreading quiet in the audience, until the heavy curtains drew magically apart, and the show began.

My Parents

I find it impossible to imagine my parents as bright young things of the nineteen-twenties, although they undoubtedly had the opportunity to be just that. My father, James Hull, was born in 1908, and my mother, Winifred Ellis, in 1914. It also seems strange that they both lived through the time of the Great War. Although my father's was largely a sea-going family, there was no talk of anyone having been lost. My father could remember standing on the beach at Newbiggin when he was a child, watching the great warships steaming out from the Tyne. By then, of course, his own father, who was forty years old at the outbreak, so too old to serve, had made the decision to leave the sea, and was usefully contributing to the efficient running of the Port of Tyne, in his capacity as master of the Commissioner's yacht.

In 1919, when he was eleven, my father started at the local grammar school. It was called Tynemouth High School, although it was in North Shields. He and his parents were living in Howdon at the time, and he was the only child who went to the grammar school from there. This, and the fact that his father was not an artisan in the shipyard, nor a coal-heaver, loading the ships that took the coal, made him something of an outsider in what was then virtually a riverside village. Matters were made worse by the fact that his mother insisted that he learn to play the piano. Luckily he was quite an athletic boy, so the fact that he went to his music lessons secretly by running along the walls at the ends of the back yards, jumping across the gateways, was not too great a problem. He became quite a proficient pianist, too.

James was an only child, so the company of other children at school was important to him. At the High School, his athleticism stood him in good stead with the other boys; as captain of cricket and captain of football, he was popular. Academically, life was a little more difficult, not because of his ability (he was bright and thoughtful, always), but because of the quality of the teachers. The school was segregated, and although male teachers were in short supply, the boys were not given the benefit of the perfectly efficient females. At that time, of course, there were few young men available to enter the profession. Those who had fought in, and survived, the War were still suffering the after-effects, so my father's memory of his teachers was that they were very old, or shell-shocked, or evil-tempered.

Violence towards the pupils was common. Canings and beatings happened every day; one teacher of French kept a cricket ball knotted into the corner of his gown, with which he hit boys' heads and knuckles if they failed to behave or learn as he wished.

Nevertheless, James enjoyed his school days. He was clever enough to make adequate progress, and sufficiently well-behaved to avoid too much punishment. He was not, however, ambitious, and as economic circumstances in the North East became more and more difficult in the 1920s, pressure from the family meant that a job with security was the imperative issue. So when he was fifteen, he left school and began to work for the London and North Eastern Railway.

His first job took him away from home to be a ticket clerk in the little station at Coldstream on the Scottish border. His mother was heart-broken, but made sure that he had a safe and respectable place to live. He lodged with two elderly sisters, both widows, who smothered him with attention and large meals, in return for which he had to perform some simple tasks; bringing in the coal, digging a huge area of garden where they grew potatoes, and most importantly, taking two glasses of stout into their bedroom at night, when they were already in bed. They believed in the medicinal properties of the beer, but feared that if they drank it before they were safe in bed, it could make them fall over.

The sojourn in Coldstream did not last long, and soon he was back, living with his parents and working at Newcastle Central Station, doing clerical work, but also evening classes in mechanical engineering, as he was more interested in the machinery than the administration of the railway. There is little else to say about his career, except that it had a period of being rather interesting towards the end of his working life, in the 1960s. By then, he was responsible for the movement in an area between Edinburgh and York, of what were called 'extraordinary and out of gauge loads'. This meant that he had to configure, organise, and often accompany, trains that carried loads which would not fit into normal wagons. Mostly, this meant large pieces of equipment, such as transformers that were going from Parsons Engineering Works to power stations in other parts of the country, or military machinery from the ordnance factory in Newcastle. For quite a while, he supervised the movement of the long rails, the installation of which meant that trains stopped saying 'clicketty-clack, clicketty-clack,' and said 'clicketty ….…….clicketty' instead. But sometimes it meant a circus, so he had to ensure that the lions were securely accommodated, the Big Top safely stowed, and once he even had to work out a route without low bridges because of a giraffe.

Going back to my father in youth, however……his love of machines at that time was satisfied by a passionate involvement with motor cycles. This had begun in childhood, when one of his mother's uncles had a bike that was, even in about 1910, quite old. It had an unusual side-car, modelled on a previous generation's Bath chair. This meant it was made of wicker and had a curved hood over it. In spite of its rather archaic appearance, my father enjoyed travelling around in it, and acquired his own motorbike as soon as he was old enough.

Thus began the most, or indeed the only, adventurous time of his life. Between the ages of seventeen and twenty he used every weekend and every bit of holiday from work to travel quite extensively. His school friend Peter May also had a motor bike, and the two young men travelled all over Northern England and much of Scotland, seeing strange ghostly faces at the upper windows of isolated moorland farmhouses, walking for miles to find replacement parts for the bikes, getting mildly electrocuted when the hem of a long wet leather coat made contact with some electrical part of the machine. They even made one foray into Europe, where the French learned under the cosh of the hidden cricket ball was severely tested in rural Belgium, with the result that they ate unidentifiable meats, and once slept in the same shed as a donkey.

Then, when my father was twenty years old, disaster struck. I have to admit that it is necessary for me to speculate on the true nature of the disaster to him, because to me it seems a relatively minor episode. It was, however, to have consequences which he felt for most of the rest of his life. He became ill with tuberculosis, and spent more than a year in a sanatorium. Then he recovered, and, until the cancer that killed him in his seventy-sixth year, never had anything worse than a bad cold again.

The gravity with which he regarded the experience of having TB is demonstrated in the manner in which I found out about it, more than fifty years after the event, shortly before he died. He spent the last weeks of his life at home, my brother and I in turn spending a week at a time to care for him. My mother had died several years earlier. Having had plenty of warning that he was dying, he had sorted out all his affairs and left the remnants of his life very neatly. One morning I had a conversation with him, which left me puzzled. He was clearly agitated and anxious, and began by grasping my wrist as if to make me pay attention.

"Elaine, there's something you don't know about me."

"Probably lots of things. Is it something special?"

"Something bad. Very bad. It's never been mentioned since I told your mother shortly after we met. But I want to tell you now."

The seriousness of his manner unnerved me.

"Tell me then."

He paused again, as if hesitating to speak to me.

"Come on, Dad, you're worrying me now."

"I'm not sure your Grandma would want anyone to know, but…I had TB. When I was twenty I spent a whole year in a sanatorium."

I waited a moment, expecting there to be more. Although I felt sorry that he had experienced this as a young man, as a piece of news it did not seem to warrant the anxiety he felt at its telling.

"Dad… it must have been very unpleasant at the time, but why are you so concerned about it now? Why should it be a secret?"

He looked at me slightly wildly, as if I had failed to understand a fundamental truth.

"Well, it's a shameful thing, isn't it." This wasn't a question.

"Not as far as I'm concerned. Does anyone think that?"

"I don't know. D'you think people don't mind about it nowadays?"

"Not in the way you seem to, no."

He turned away and lay down on his bed again. I felt that there was nothing more for him to say; he was preoccupied by the point of view I had expressed.

Since that conversation, I have occasionally returned to the idea of that shame, which was so deeply ingrained in him that it could only be revealed as a deathbed confession. At first, I remembered that in my own childhood there were ailments that carried a stigma of dirt and poverty. Once, to my mother's horror and disgust, I had an attack of impetigo. An unmistakable sore appeared on my thigh, a kind of blister, which broke in the middle, formed a yellow crusty edge, and was excruciatingly painful to touch. She regarded the place anxiously, apparently wondering whether it could possibly be a respectable allergy, or the result of a fall. Then she noticed a tiny but similar lesion starting on my cheek. Treatment was necessary, but, very unusually, not from Dr. Yeoman. Instead, I was taken to the pharmacy, where behind the counter worked a woman who, years before, had been one of my grandfather's chambermaids. She clearly understood the problem, and swiftly whisked me into a back room where the merits of various ointments could be discussed out of public sight.

So, for a while, I believed that the problem posed to my father by his youthful illness was one in which TB was seen as a disease suffered only by slum dwellers, dirty people who were not respectable. I had difficulty reconciling this with the knowledge that such figures as D.H. Lawrence and Robert Louis Stevenson had suffered and indeed died of it without loss of reputation, and that operas had been written around characters such as Mimi and Violetta.

Much later, when time lent me an objective distance to think about my parents and how they conducted their lives, I began to wonder whether there was a significance to the conversation my father had instigated, which he had presumed I would know about. Reading one day about men who had wanted to serve in the Second World War, but who had been turned down because of various health problems, I realised that my father's brush with what was then a dangerous, even deadly, disease, would have rendered him exempt from service. This then was the explanation for his not having fought in that war.

Although I was born in 1945, and the effects of that terrible conflict must have been present in the memories and emotions of every adult, it was rarely mentioned in our family. There was the odd funny story, such as about Aunt Lizzie taking out her false teeth and putting a cushion on her head when she went in the air-raid shelter. Indeed in our back garden there was a hollow in the lawn, the result of filling in the hole left by an Anderson shelter. Ration books were still very much a part of life, and shopping for food was referred to as 'going for the rations' (that is, when not using the Geordie phrase 'doing the messages'). But, other than this, in our family it was not a topic of conversation. If the TB were the reason for his lack of involvement, my father would have been in a terribly awkward position. He was a fairly young man, and would have seemed to neighbours and acquaintances even younger than his thirty-four years, as a newly married man in 1942. But he was deeply ashamed of the disease that had proved to be his protector. I now suspect that life was made difficult for him, as it was for many men who for one reason or another did not get sent away to fight, but the shame was such that he could not offer the redemptive explanation.

Consequently, my father became somewhat reclusive. Certainly, he did not dislike other people, but much of his behaviour for the first twenty years or so of his marriage indicated a caution, an uncertainty about coming into contact with others, and as a result he did very little outside the family. Month after month, year after year, his weekly routine was unswervingly the same. Weekdays he went to work, Sunday afternoons we all went to visit his mother. On Wednesday evenings he had tea with his mother. That was it.

Some aspects of this showed an almost obsessive desire to be at home. Coming home for his midday meal, for instance, involved a twenty-minute train journey in each direction, and twenty minutes at home to eat a proper dinner of meat, two veg and a pudding. Our parents' social life was meagre to say the least. They had two friends, Ross and Florence, who invited them to the Round Table Annual Dance. The local swimming club had an annual dance also, which they attended. Until about 1955 these were the only times my father left the house except for family outings and to go to work. Then when I was about ten years old he started to go to church occasionally.

This gives a picture of an unattractively dull man, which could not be further from the truth. He was intelligent and humorous, in that way Geordie men have, loving dreadful puns and their own wit. He was widely read, and accomplished (the piano lessons had the effect that he could play proficiently and enjoyed doing so). Most conspicuously, he was remarkably good-looking all his life; all in all, a man who should have been easy and confident in social circumstances. In part, my mother kept up an explanation for his quiet life by saying 'Jim is shy', but he hadn't been shy as the accomplished schoolboy, nor as the young man travelling on his motorbike. Even in 1938, when he and my mother met, he may have been affected by the need for secrecy about that incident in his past, but he was not so unsociable as he became during and after the war. They met at a badminton club. Both competent players, they had friends there who existed after 1945 only as names in occasional conversations. I believe that the strange prejudice and shame about a disease, and then the difficulty of being seen as a man protected or cowardly during the war, forced him into a secretive, private, inward-looking life.

In his old age, in retirement, he had a few years in which he behaved differently. After my mother's death he was afraid of his loneliness, and sought company in a way that was courageously different from the previous many years. He went to a weekly lunch club for retired businessmen, although strictly speaking he did not qualify. He took elderly people for outings in his car; although he was older than many of them, he did not seem so. He played bowls with some skill and lots of enthusiasm. He became a churchwarden. Once he had overcome, to a certain extent, his reticence about contact with others, he was regarded as kindly and courteous, a natural gentleman. But still, until that day not long before he died, he regarded himself as a man with a shameful secret, a man whom others would shun if they knew. I sometimes wonder whether my surprise and attempted reassurance made him feel better, or whether perhaps it gave him a sense that so many opportunities had been missed because of his fear. Or perhaps he simply did not believe me.

All of his many attractive qualities, not least his good looks, were appreciated in a rather stunned way by my mother, for she was in her own way flawed. Once, when I was seven or eight, she and I sat together looking through some old family snapshots. We came to one of herself and my father's cousin, Peggy, taken when they were in their mid-twenties. Peggy, in spite of having one eye that looked at you and one that looked over your head, was quite a jolly looking girl, with wavy blonde hair and a cheeky smile. My mother, Winnie, short and very slim (in her view skinny, because she had no bosom) wore round spectacles and had a broken front tooth. My mother looked at this photograph, sighed, and said, "What did your Dad see in me, I was so plain?" With the honesty of childhood I said, "I don't know." Talking more to herself than to me she said, "Of course, he spent most of his time with his mother."

Loving my Grandma as I did this sounded perfectly feasible to me. Growing older with this vague explanation tucked into my semi-conscious, consistent with the notion of his 'shyness', I thought little more about their relationship. In retrospect, it is obvious that they had a deep and abiding affection for one another, but this had on each side an element of gratitude, hers because she regarded herself as unworthy in a variety of ways, his, less obviously, because she accepted the man with the shameful secret and loved him.

This unworthiness of my mother's became a very central and crucial factor in my own life. Where did it arise? I came to realise that it had its origins in relationships she formed in childhood, both within her family and with a crucial group of friends. She was next to youngest in a large family; two half-brothers, Harry and Jimmy (who was drowned from a fishing boat when a teenager), her own brother Geoffrey, her sister Marjorie, herself and the youngest, Hilda.

Of the three girls, maybe she was the least attractive in appearance. Marjorie was taller, with neat pert features, and a slightly feline smile, Hilda small, pretty and curly-haired. It was the spectacles, present from early childhood, and the tooth, broken when she was fourteen, which made her self-conscious and awkward about her appearance.

In personality, she was perhaps the quietest, even slightly introspective. Hilda was fun, irresistibly giggly, the slightly indulged youngest, and always the one my mother felt closest to. With Marjorie, more volatile and quarrelsome, she had a difficult relationship, often at odds. They fell out seriously when I was a toddler, and had more than twenty years of estrangement. I think my memory of this quarrel pre-dates even that of buying my brother in the doctor's surgery. Marjorie and her husband Len lived in Wembley, and my parents and I went to stay with them, in those days a long and quite exciting distance away from Newcastle. In order for us all to be accommodated, my cousins, Frank and Brenda, and I all had to sleep in the same bed. Because I was the youngest, the adults decided the best arrangement would be for me to sleep at the foot of the bed. This gave the two older children the opportunity to poke me with their feet, for what felt like all night. Something happened the next morning (not in any way related to my sleeping arrangements), and we left the house with my mother in high dudgeon. I remember the emphatic rhythm of her feet as we marched towards the station, me swinging ignominiously between my parents, unable to keep up.

My Uncle Geoff was a bit of a mystery to me. I could not reconcile the stories of childhood pranks with the little grey man I knew, in appearance a cross between Charlie Chaplin and Hitler, but drawn pale and misty. I saw him about once a year, at Christmastime, when we went for tea with him, his quiet little wife and my three cousins. The surviving half-brother Harry was quite a bit older, and moved away from the North East years before I was born. I have no real memory of him.

The family led a somewhat unusual life, living as they did in pubs and hotels. The location and quality of the establishments improved through my grandfather's working life. At the time when my mother was born, they lived in a rather modest pub near the station at Percy Main, the Percy Arms. This was a smoke-darkened stone building, Victorian railway architecture, a drinking place only, without accommodation.

Soon my grandfather's work took them to the coast, into another small pub on Front Street, Cullercoats, then just along the same road, to the Bay Hotel, an attractive and substantial building overlooking Cullercoats Bay. Finally, the move was made into Whitley Bay where for a number of years, I think until his retirement, my grandfather ran the Victoria Hotel. In those days this was quite a classy establishment, catering for those holiday-makers who considered themselves a cut above seaside bed-and-breakfast places, or boarding houses. The very best hotel was the Rex, on the sea front, but the Vic had a mirrored dining room, a billiards room and a ballroom. My mother enjoyed this time, the constant ebb and flow of guests, the bustle of lots of staff, the relatively palatial living quarters for the family, and the busy-ness of the bars, although officially the children were not allowed to set foot in the public rooms. Here is a hint of the temper that I saw later in my grand-father. My Aunt Hilda told me that although they did venture into parts of the building where they were not allowed, it was always in great fear of discovery, because they knew, boys and girls alike, that if they were caught they would be beaten.

Yet it was here that my quiet uncle, Geoff, as a boy, frequently courted trouble. One day, my grandfather, working in the lounge of the hotel, became aware that a small amused crowd was gathering on the forecourt. When he stepped outside it was to find young Geoffrey, stark naked and swinging from the lamp over the door. On another occasion, the child found his way into the cellar. Here, the spirits were stored in large barrel-shaped pottery jars, each with a cup under the tap to catch the drips. Geoff drained them all, a sufficient quantity to render him unconscious and in need of a stomach pump. Having recovered and come home, he made his way into that same cellar, where he stirred all the beer barrels with a stick normally used to stir bleach into the vats where the linen was washed. Hundreds of gallons of beer had to be poured down the drain.

Life was interesting and enjoyable here, but amongst it my mother grew to regard herself as the least attractive, least intelligent, least interesting of the children. She performed averagely at school, both admiring and jealous of Hilda, who went to the grammar school. Afterwards they both trained as hairdressers. I think Marjorie did some secretarial work until she married, and Geoff, throughout his working life, was an electrician in the shipyards. So when my mother acquired and ran her own business, she was in a sense the most successful of the siblings, although she never saw herself as such.

Her salon, or 'the shop' as she called it, was on John Street, in Cullercoats, not far from the school where I would later go. She worked there alone for several years, selling up only after my brother was born. As a baby and toddler, I had been content to play in a corner while she worked, but she could not manage this with two children. So 'the shop' was gone, and my mother never thought of herself as having been a businesswoman.

Much of her poor self-esteem was centred on a group of friends, Hilda's originally, who remained in my mother's life after Hilda had grown up, married and moved away to Yorkshire. Central to this group were two sisters, Margery and Nancy Smith. There was another sister, Margaret, but she was younger, and figured in the group only later when they were adults. The Smith sisters were strikingly pretty, actually really beautiful. They were also friendly, sociable, and genuinely pleasant, and grew up to be the core of a fluctuating group of friends centred on Cullercoats Swimming Club. My mother was in this group, but never felt herself to be truly a part of it. The fault lay, not in the way anyone behaved towards her, but in her own estimation of herself. Because she felt less pretty, less sociable, less relaxed in company, she also felt marginalised. Although it was plain that she made a number of potentially rewarding friendships within the group, there was often more pain than pleasure in it for her. From time to time someone new would come along, join the club, and be welcomed into what my mother saw as the inner circle. If such a person had a normal amount of self-confidence, she would be quickly and obviously accepted. This would mean that, at one and the same time, my mother would hate her and long to be her friend. I remember one such woman, a relaxed, friendly and slightly eccentric person, who had two daughters named Topsy and Tansy, unusual in the 1950s. In public, my mother invited this woman for coffee, chatted to her at the club, and was generally normally friendly. In private she poured scorn and derision on the names of the unwitting children.

She put herself into an uncomfortable, indeed untenable situation. She longed to be liked, accepted, even perhaps healed, by these women. Then whenever she formed a close enough friendship with one of them so that they spent time together, she could not resist the kind of gossiping which undermined the friendship. She was never overtly horrible about anyone, so often it would take several months or even years for the friend to drift away, feeling uncomfortably that she had been drawn by my mother into a slightly bitchy disloyalty.

The withdrawn nature of my father's life added to her isolation. Most of the other husbands regularly used the clubhouse, played on the beach with the children, taught us to swim, and had their own friendships. My father rarely set foot in the place. The reason given was that he could not swim; I did not question this as a child, although it was apparent even then to me that swimming was an unimportant aspect of the life of the club.

All of this made her quietly but implacably angry. Alongside maintaining a façade of friendliness, in part genuine, she needed a weapon with which to beat these women who would not, could not, cure her self-hatred. Suddenly she had one, an asset which none of them owned, a tool to demonstrate her superiority, which she used, quietly, relentlessly, and ruthlessly. It was me; she had the Cleverest Child.

Health Matters

Until I was six and a half years old, I lived the paradoxical life of being a naturally healthy and robust child who was ill. The whooping cough that I do not remember, but which, according to my mother, nearly killed me, left me with a susceptibility to problems in my nose and throat. By the time I was four, this had settled into a chronic infection of the adenoids and nasal sinuses. I can't have been a very attractive child. Breathing through my mouth was the norm for me, my nose exuded so much yellow mucus that I had to use my father's large handkerchiefs, and swallowed catarrh meant that not infrequently I woke in the night to be sick. Nevertheless, it was another two years or so before the problem was tackled with any determination, and in the meantime I was dosed with black, liquorice-flavoured, cough mixtures, I had my head steamed over bowls of Friars Balsam and my chest liberally rubbed with camphorated oil. I must have smelled pretty unusual too.

This was one aspect of life in which I did not thoroughly approve of my Grandma. She insisted on using on me ancient remedies that were at best ineffectual, at worst possibly dangerous. They were certainly unpleasant. If I were sufficiently incautious as to mention that my stomach had been unsettled she would force upon me a disgusting concoction called Gregory's

Powders. No matter how I attempted to dissuade her, insisting that I felt fine, was completely recovered, out would come a glass with an inch of milk in it and a substantial quantity of greyish dust floating on the surface. I had to swallow all of it. It was horribly bitter, and the undissolved particles stuck all over the inside of my mouth, prolonging the unpleasantness. I could feel my face involuntarily contracting into a grimace and my eyes watering. It was so vile that, even in the face of much previous experience, I always thought that I should have the benefit of some significant improvement, some miraculous glow suffusing my whole being, but of course it never made any difference.

Another horrible method was practised on me if the customary nasal infection spread to my chest, which it did all too frequently. The first sign of a fruity cough would mean the goose grease treatment. From a jar of this smelly slime, which was kept in the pantry, a handful would be spread over a piece of red flannel cloth, slapped onto my chest, and tied there with a crepe bandage. Then my woollen vest would go on over the top, and there it would stay, until the cough abated, or I went home, whichever were the sooner. My mother had a slightly more up-to-date attitude to medication, but she never actually told my Grandma that the goose grease would not work.

In both houses I was dosed with a variety of tonics, several of which were actually quite enjoyable. The Welfare State provided delicious orange juice for babies, and after I outgrew my own entitlement I was given my brother's, as he was plainly strong and healthy, and I was not. I actually liked cod-liver oil, and willingly swallowed a spoonful of that every morning. Even so, several variants were tried, perhaps on the assumption that if you pay more for a version that has been mucked about in some way, it will be more effective. One that I enjoyed was Scott's Emulsion, invented for the benefit of people who couldn't stomach cod-liver oil in its unadulterated form. It was lovely sticky white stuff with a unique flavour, slightly oily, slightly sweet. Best of all was Virol, described on its label as cod-liver oil and malt. It was dark and treacly, tasted fudgy and beery, really delicious.

Although I was quite happy to drink plenty of milk unmodified, I was encouraged to drink even more in the form of Ovaltine, which was given to me at breakfast and at bedtime. After a while I developed an appalling rash, my body covered with inflamed white spots the size of an old penny, which itched unbearably. It was a mystery, which Doctor Yeoman eventually solved by saying that I was allergic to the massive doses of malt I was getting in the combination of Virol and Ovaltine. So these treats stopped, and sure enough the spots went away. Myself, at first I thought they were fleabites, but of course my mother would not have such a suggestion voiced. There was no way in her opinion that I could have been exposed to fleas, but I had seen the same thing on the children who lived on the farm up the lane from Grandma's house, and I had carried their old cat around in spite of being told not to, in case I got fleas. In any case, when Dr. Yeoman gave his diagnosis I believed him. I regretted the Virol and the Ovaltine though.

Another mysterious ailment afflicted me, in the form of extensive tooth decay. The mystery is how I came by it. I didn't eat sweets other than very moderately, sugar was still rationed, I wasn't allowed fizzy drinks, which my mother regarded as common, and I brushed my teeth night and morning. Nevertheless, one by one, my back teeth developed holes, started to ache, and had to be removed. Because they were my milk teeth, and would therefore be replaced before long anyway, no attempt was made to save them by filling. Thank goodness, as the process of taking them out was bad enough. The dentist was Mr. Dewar, whose surgery was conveniently across the road from Grandma's. I think part of the convenience was that my mother could be largely uninvolved with the process. I could be left at The Crest, and Grandma would take me, and try to deal with the trauma.

I would be taken, in fear and trembling after the first occasion, as I had learned what to expect, my aching molars were perfunctorily inspected, then the torture would begin. For extractions, although the operation was done with a general anaesthetic, or 'gas' as it was called, Mr. Dewar wanted to ensure that the child would not struggle. So you were made to lie down on a leather-covered table with thick, buckled, straps at the four corners. Next, wrists and ankles were tightly strapped down. Only then was the horrible black rubber mask clamped over your face, followed by the dreadful whirling descent into blackness. Waking, to the ironish taste of blood in the mouth, and a few hours of shaking legs and vomiting, was nevertheless a relief. The process was over until the next time.

I must have been quite an easy patient for Mr. Dewar, in spite of my dread, because of course I had already learned stoicism. I could put into practice that knowledge that if I could just make myself wait, the ordeal would pass, and that in any case screaming brought no relief. On one or two occasions, in the waiting room with my Grandma, we witnessed screaming children being carried away untreated because their behaviour rendered them unmanageable. Once, my own brother was one of these children. I regarded them with a mixture of envy and pity. The pity was because I knew that they would be back, the envy not because they had avoided the treatment, but because they could scream, in the unselfconscious innocence of an unencumbered childhood, and with some confidence of being heard.

Eventually, it became apparent that medicine, camphor and tonics were not going to cure the problem of my coughs and infected sinuses. The bones of my face ached to the extent that even having my hair brushed was painful. One morning I woke from a fitful sleep and found that my view of the world had been reduced to a blurred slit. In the night my face had swollen so hugely that my eyes could barely open. My mother held me over the wash-basin in the bathroom and bathed my face until I could see, but, as she did so, a sudden rush of blood and pus poured from my nostrils.

A consultation with Mr. Dalrymple, an ear, nose and throat specialist at Preston Hospital in North Shields resulted in the decision that as well as a course of strong antibiotics, I would need an operation to wash out my sinuses. This is a minor procedure of course, done to adults while they sit up and watch what is going on, but I was unusually young to need it, and it was decided that I should be admitted to the hospital, stay a couple of days, and have it done under general anaesthetic.

There was a week or two to wait. Meanwhile, I went to school as usual. Mrs. Douglas suggested that I choose a book from the ones we had in the classroom to take to the hospital with me, and I picked out Noddy in Toytown. If only I had realised that I would need several. My mother came in to school to talk to Mrs. Huntley about my absence, and I was brought into her office to share in the conversation. Already, as a result of my sacking from the milk job, I was cautious of the head mistress, and doubtful of her judgement, although I could not have explained this at the time. My mother told her how unwell I had been for so long, and explained that I would be away from school for some days when the operation took place. Mrs. Huntley's broad face was almost as immobile and expressionless as usual, except for a fleeting cloud of irritation. In those days it was quite unusual for a parent to come into school, and she apparently thought my mother was making an unnecessary fuss.

"Are we sure this treatment is strictly necessary?" she asked. "All children get colds."

"Well it isn't really a cold Elaine's got," said my mother, "she can't breathe properly through her nose at all."

"Have you tried this?" the woman asked, taking out her own handkerchief and thrusting it under my nose. Such air as I could squeeze through my constricted nostrils carried with it a trace of the familiar smell of camphor. For a moment, compared to this monumental inability to understand what was being said to her, I felt ineffably wise.

The time came for me to go into the hospital. I was nervous, but everyone I had met there so far had been kind to me, so I arrived with my mother expecting the experience to be bearable. The first snag was that the children's ward was full, and as my stay was to be a short one, I was to be put to bed in a women's ward. It was a huge, open, white space; white walls with tall high windows reflecting a white cloudy sky, shiny floor stretching into the distance. Along each wall, a row of ten or twelve white beds, with their neatly tucked pale inhabitants, and at the side of each a white cupboard. No chairs. In those days, when you arrived you got into bed, and mostly that is where you stayed. I felt small, particularly as the beds were so high that my view along the expanse of the ward was largely below their level.

Next, I have on my nightie, I am sitting up in one of the high beds, and my mother is leaving me. I see her walking away, through the door at the end of the room, a small dark figure in the whiteness of the space. Probably she is upset at leaving me there, but I cannot tell, as she does not turn to look back. Probably someone has told me how long I will be here, but I have forgotten, and in any case, when you are in agony, a minute is an age.

Although my mother has gone, there are other women in the ward who have a motherly feeling towards me, and believe that by treating me nicely, they can overcome my shock. Questions start to bounce across the room.

"What's your name, pet?"

"How old are you?"

"What's wrong with you, hinny?"

One woman, more mobile and more determined than the others, makes it across the ward to put her arms around me, and I am speechless with relief when a nurse comes to chase her back into bed. To my surprise, this nurse has a wheelchair which I am briskly lifted into, and whirled off along corridors.

"I know you can walk," she says, "but this is quicker, and your mam hasn't brought you any slippers."

I feel let down that my mother has not equipped me properly, but 'mam' is common, you should say 'mummy', so I know she doesn't really have the authority to comment. We arrive at a room where I am weighed and measured, and where I wee in a pot behind a curtain and some of my wee is taken away in a bottle. Then we pretend to have a bit of fun having my hands and face washed, and I am taken back to the bed.

I am frightened of the other women. I do not want them to talk to me, and in any case it is embarrassing to see some of their loose old bodies in their pink nighties; they are strangers and should not be revealed to me in this way. So

I turn on my tummy with my Noddy in Toytown book which I have brought with me from school. By now, aged six, I can read proficiently, and it takes me about half an hour to read from cover to cover, so I read it again, more slowly. To my relief, it seems to be bedtime, although how this is decided when you are in bed already, I don't know. The lights turn dim and blue, and the snoring starts.

I believe I slept little during that night. Certainly I was aware of movement at regular intervals; a nurse in soft shoes gliding back and forth with bed linen, a new inhabitant for a bed at the furthest end brought in moaning audibly, all the creaks, groans and snorts of twenty women sleeping or trying to sleep. Eventually, at the end of an age, the lights turned back to yellow, the sky outside the windows paled, and tea and porridge started to be delivered around the ward. I wasn't hungry, but was nevertheless disappointed when I wasn't given any. Instead, some medicine in a little plastic cup, 'because you are going for your operation.' Then I read Noddy in Toytown again. I quite enjoyed it, but by now I was anxious about the fact that it was my only book. I had no idea how long I would need to keep hiding in its pages, and it would have been good to lose myself in something else. I had found that the simple little adventures of Noddy and his friends did take my mind away temporarily from the fears and discomforts of real life.

A cheery looking man appeared at the side of my bed, pushing another bed on wheels. "Jump on," he said, "we're going for a ride." Then there was another rush around the corridors, and in a lift. I had been told to lie down, so all I saw was the procession of lights along the ceiling. I was feeling slightly sleepy by now, presumably as a result of swallowing the draught in the plastic cup, but I thought because of my restless, sleepless night.

The next part, I find hard to explain or understand, given that I was a little child on the way for an operation, albeit a minor one. The trolley with me on it was pushed into an operating theatre, and I was left there alone. I say it was an operating theatre because above my head, and I was lying obediently on my back looking upwards, was a very large circular light. It had a shiny chrome reflective border, in which I could see a small distorted image of myself.

I lay there for a long time, maybe an hour or more, the creeping cloud of fear and alienation from reality gradually overcoming me. Perhaps there was an assumption that I was asleep, or at least drowsy from the drug, and would be unaware of my surroundings or the waiting. This became more and more impossible, however. I had not been to the toilet since that time the night before when my urine sample had been taken, and the need to go became uncomfortable, then imperative. For some time, maybe ten more long minutes, I hung on to the belief that soon someone would come to collect me. I sat up, gingerly and in serious discomfort by now, and looked around the room to see if there were any signs that I had not been completely abandoned. More white walls, a long white bench with a steel sink in it, and white double doors each with a porthole window. As well as being empty of people, the room was silent. I lay down again, now breathing in shallow gasps of pain and anxiety. My every emotion was at odds with my circumstances. I was a child naturally inclined to obedience, and moreover taught to be so; I had that deeply rooted knowledge that I did not scream or the agony would be prolonged. Also, I knew that certain standards of behaviour were expected of me, and wetting the bed was a filthy, babyish and undisciplined act. So I forced myself to lie still, desperately hoping for someone to open the door and rescue me. The gasping breaths became audible, tears ran from my eyes into my ears and the discomfort turned to pain. Suddenly I was crying aloud, crying noisily, howling. I knew I was screaming and screaming, and I was shocked and ashamed but I couldn't stop.

Within moments, the door opened and a nurse came in, not cross and scornful as I expected, but concerned.

"I need the lav," I gasped, and she picked me off the trolley, and carried me (to my absolute astonishment; I could not remember having been carried by anyone, ever) and quickly deposited me on a lavatory in a room close by. The physical relief was overwhelming, and I cried again, partly out of shame, that I had been unable to summon the help that was so readily available in a more dignified manner.

Afterwards I was carried back to my trolley, but now she stayed with me, and within minutes I was wheeled away again. At the next destination, a man came to speak to me. All I could see of him was a pair of blue eyes above a cloth mask, but the eyes looked friendly. He informed me that he was going to help me to go to sleep, and asked me if I could count to ten. Insulted, I replied that I could count to any number, and he told me ten would do. A rubbery mask descended over my face, and I began to count. The sudden shadowy whirling sensation, familiar from my visits to the dentist, began. I remember thinking very clearly that I hadn't even got to four, and then I was awake again in the long white ward.

I felt pretty bad, but the memory of my ordeal on the trolley was so strong; it was as if the pain and subsequent relief had happened in the past two minutes, so my current discomfort was bearable. There was pain in the bones of my face. I was accustomed to that. I felt rather sick, and inclined to lie very still to avoid throwing up. Then I was aware that my nostrils were tightly packed, but as I had not used them for breathing for some years, this made little difference to me.

Slowly, I became aware that I was not alone. I could hear quiet breathing beside me. In a flash it occurred to me that the operation was over, and my mother was here to take me home. So I quickly turned to see her. At the side of the bed sat the woman who served in the chemist's shop, the one who had known my mother since she was a girl, and who would in a year or two give antiseptic powder for my impetigo. I was disappointed, but somehow not surprised. I was learning another chapter in the story that tells you that when you suffer, you are alone.

"Where is my mummy?" I asked. I realised this sounded churlish, and I was asking out of curiosity rather than need, but she answered a question I had not asked.

"They won't let her come until you're ready to go home. You would only get upset if she came to visit you, then went away again."

This had a ring of truth, and I had neither the logic nor the strength to refute it.

"I'll tell her you're alright. I've brought you some Lucozade from the shop," she continued.

"Thank you." I liked Lucozade, but I was aware that there was a lie somewhere in what she had said. Also, I did not need Lucozade, I needed another book or two. Remembering this, and wanting her to go, as she was serving no purpose other than to make me feel embarrassed that I couldn't think of anything more to say, I'm ashamed to remember that I took Noddy out from under the pillow, and started again at the beginning.

"Bye 'bye then, pet," she said, patted me on the head, and left. I read on, through the whole book twice more, no longer taking in a single word, just using it to keep the world away from me. I didn't know her name, and I didn't think she and my mother were friends. The women who were her friends I called Auntie, though I knew they weren't.

I was desperately thirsty. The clock on the wall told me it was after midday, and I had had no breakfast, not even a drink of water, indeed nothing since a cup of milk just before the blue lights came on the night before. There was a glass on the shelf of my cupboard, so I managed to sit up on the side of the bed, open the Lucozade bottle and pour a good slosh into the glass. I swallowed this hurriedly, poured and drank some more, and settled back in my bed. Immediately, I felt very much worse than before, my head swam, my stomach churned and heaved, and all the Lucozade spurted out over the white bedspread. In answer to a call from one of the other beds, a stocky dark-haired nurse appeared at my side. For the first time, someone was impatient and cross.

"Whatever did you do that for?" she grumbled, "You know you shouldn't have anything to eat or drink 'til you've got over your anaesthetic. That was very, very naughty."

Of course, I had not known. In common with many things, I had not been told, perhaps because I was on an adult's ward where they were unused to dealing with a child. I was about to discover something else I had not known. She lifted me down from the bed, and began to remove the sheets.

"Go and have a wash," she said over her shoulder, nodding in the direction of the door at the end of the ward. I walked shakily in that direction, and saw on the wall a small white washbasin with long-handled taps. It had no plug, so I let the taps run and splashed the water over my face and hands. Luckily the vomit had all gone onto the bedclothes so my nightie was still clean.

From behind me a gentle voice said, "What are you doing, little one?" It was Mr. Dalrymple, the doctor who was in charge of me here. I recognised his stethoscope and a tie he wore with very bright blue and yellow diagonal stripes.

"She told me to have a wash. I had some Lucozade and I was sick," I replied.

"Why don't you use the bathroom?" he asked.

"I don't know where it is." Suddenly it became obvious to me that of course there would be a bathroom. The place was strange and unlike a house, but certain basic things would have to be there. He took my hand and led me a few steps to where an open archway led to a row of little rooms each with a basin on one wall and a bath on the other. At the end of the row were several toilet cubicles. With a mixture of gratitude, embarrassment and anger that no-one had taken the simple step of showing me this place, I slipped into one of the little bathrooms and shut the door. When enough time had passed for him to have gone, I came out, went luxuriously to the lavatory, and then washed my hands copiously with warm water and yellow soap that smelled of tar. Then I went back to my bed, which was also newly clean.

Mr. Dalrymple was moving along the ward, speaking to a patient here and there. He listened to chests, looked into mouths and eventually came to me.

"You're all done then, " he said. "Let's get that cotton wool out." He had a pair of fat tweezers in his hand with which he gripped the substance that was stuffing my nostrils. As he pulled, a substantial quantity of bloodstained dressing came out. It felt to me as if the whole of the inside of my head was being dragged out. The pulling went on for longer than would seem possible given the small size of my nose. Some time later, when I heard in school about the ancient Egyptians pulling the brains of dead people out using hooks up the nose, I thought "I know what that feels like, and I wasn't even dead."

After a while it stopped. The doctor said, "That's fine, take a deep breath for me," so I opened my mouth and did so.
He laughed. "No, I mean through your nose."
I shut my mouth, thought about it, and breathed deeply. A great jet of what felt like icy air rushed into my head and made my eyes water. Instantly, I opened my mouth again in order to breathe in the way that was normal for me.
"Excellent," said the doctor, "That's done the trick. You'll soon get used to it."

Sometime later that afternoon I went home. My mother unexpectedly came through the door where she had disappeared so long ago. Was it really only one day? I had learned so much of mistrust, and self-reliance, and how the inside of a book can keep horrible things at bay. Nowadays I have a granddaughter, aged six. I imagine her experiencing the things that happened to me, and my heart breaks.

My mother, who had walked away from me without looking back, took me home on the bus. I was pleased to be there and in time I became accustomed to breathing through my nose. I was well, 'full of beans' as my father described it, and I liked it.

Home

Of course, during my childhood there was the usual succession of seasons, including blue summer days in the sun, when the dry yellow sand in Cullercoats Bay was too hot for the feet. There were golden, smoky, autumn mornings when the road to school was through crisp drifts of fallen leaves. We stared into rock pools ruffled by warm breezes, collected the crimson handprints of sycamore leaves to stick into scrapbooks, and played out of doors endlessly. But much of my recollection of those early years at home is of cold, the grey gloom of November around my birthday, or bright hard frosts of midwinter. Many mornings began with the crystal feathers and icy etched skeleton leaves of Jack Frost's paintings on the panes of my bedroom windows, though it snowed rarely on the coast of that grey-green sea.

Daily life at our house in Newton Avenue started with the battle of the fireplace. The small coal fire that sputtered there was the only source of heat and hot water. My father suspected that there was a way of banking up the fire at night that would keep it alive for the morning, but he never achieved this, largely because it required a frighteningly expensive amount of coal to be piled on, which would probably just burn up while we were asleep, and disappear.

Therefore, his ritual of fire-lighting. This began with the cleaning of the grate. A metal pan underneath caught most of the ashes, then the residue was scraped out with a small shovel. Next there was the re-cycling of yesterday's Evening Chronicle. A double page was rolled tightly, then curled into a loose knot. The rolling had to start at a corner and proceed diagonally or the resulting coil would be too thick to light easily. Three or four of these were piled in the fireplace and surrounded by a wigwam of sticks, and a few small pieces of coal. One match was used to light a coloured spill, a long sliver of thin wood, a clutch of which stood in a card tube on the hearth. The spill was more efficient than a match, as it burned longer, so it was applied to the paper in several places. If the paper lit the sticks, and they burned long enough to start the coal, all was well, but sometimes all the paper would burn away without success, and the whole process had to be started again. Meanwhile, the rest of the family were dressing with chattering teeth, and having the sort of wash in lukewarm water that my mother described as 'a lick and a promise'.

My brother Kit, like many children an arsonist manqué, wanted to light the fire himself, and sometimes was allowed to try, with my 'supervision'. It was more difficult than we could understand. Rolling the newspaper tightly was tricky, so we abandoned that in favour of crumpled lumps, which burned in seconds and left the coal untouched. Then somehow my brother learned of a trick, which we tried while our father was out of the room. Having got a bit of flame in the sticks, we spread a sheet of the newspaper over the front of the fireplace. It had to be held in place at each corner, and because Kit wanted to do it all himself, he held the upper corners with his hands and the lower ones with his feet. This was not easy, as he was still quite small. Immediately there was an interesting roar as behind the paper we could see a minor inferno building up. The rush of air as it was drawn through the restricted space of the grate fed a gratifying amount of flame. Soon the coal would catch and by the time Dad came back we would have a good fire going. Kit turned to grin at me, his concentration lapsed, and the sheet of newspaper burst into flames. Fortunately, as he screamed and shook it away from his hands, it was whisked up the chimney, leaving a miserably smoking pile of half-consumed sticks and no fire.

For me, the attempts to achieve some warmth in the morning had begun earlier, even the night before, when I spread all of my clothes under the eiderdown on my bed. Thus, when I woke in the morning, the clothes were warm, and I could drag them one by one under the covers and be fully dressed before I got out of bed. Personal hygiene was of secondary consideration. This cast an interesting reflection on my mother's attitude to correctness. Washing and bathing of oneself took place in the bathroom. Our bathroom was unheated, in other words freezing, so we spent as little time in it as possible. Splash the face and hands, brush the teeth, get out of there. When I went along the street to call for my friend Maureen to go to school, I would often find her standing in the kitchen sink having her legs thoroughly washed up to pants level by her mother. This practice was looked down on by my mother; it was 'common'. So we were more respectable, but probably less clean. I didn't realise it at the time, but of course washing in the kitchen was reminiscent of a time when there was no bathroom inside the house. Such a situation was not to be implied in our household, by word or deed.

Our parents had bought this house in 1945, in the last months of the war, and moved in just before I was born. On the edge of an estate of six similar roads, with the sea-front, the railway station and the beginning of the countryside all within a few hundred yards, it was an attractive-looking semi, with a bay window at the front, and a garden big enough to play in at the back. They paid £620 for it, and were convinced it was the best house in the neighbourhood. This was because the builder who had developed the estate in the 1930s had reserved this particular plot for himself, although the war changed his circumstances and he never lived in the house. It was different because it had a slightly larger amount of land, which meant that it had a garage and a path down the side to give access to the back garden, whereas all the other houses had one or the other. This back garden had two lawns on different levels, broad steps leading from the top one to the bottom. At the sides were flower borders, one of which was mine. I grew candytuft, lupins and marigolds with an ease that I now regard as suspicious. Someone else must have been interfering with my plot. At the side of the bottom lawn my father had a small greenhouse, where he grew tomatoes and chrysanthemums. Behind a low brick wall at the front of the house was a smaller garden, mostly rose beds with a circular red gravel path. This seemed to be more my mother's domain. She kept it tidy, rather in the same way as she operated indoors, so the whole appearance of the front was one of neatness and orderliness. In my earliest memories of the house, all the woodwork was grained, which meant that it was painted and varnished to resemble the appearance of the wood that was under the paint and varnish.

Inside, there were three rooms downstairs, the dining room at the back, where we mostly lived, the front room, used hardly at all, and a small kitchen. Upstairs, three bedrooms, the chilly bathroom and a separate lavatory. There must have been hundreds of thousands of houses just like it all over the country. Our parents were very satisfied with it, and stayed there for the rest of their lives, in the case of my mother until 1977, and my father until 1983. They both died there.

Partly because they both liked the house, partly because there was never a surfeit of money, and partly because my mother always had a slightly angry, matyred attitude that told her she did not deserve better, they never made substantial changes. After a while the rather heavy front door, which made the hallway dark as it had only a small stained-glass window, was replaced by one with frosted glass panels. The grained woodwork was painted cream and turquoise. The fireplaces were filled and gas fires put in place (oh frabjous day). Otherwise, it remained a house of the 1930s. One aspect of this (apart from the continued absence of central heating), fills me with the mixture of anger, frustration and amusement that became my frequent reaction to my mother once I was no longer a child. In around 1960, some local authority grants became available which could be claimed by private householders to pay half the cost of upgrading basic facilities in their homes. Because these houses all had tiny kitchens with no space for modern appliances, neighbours to the left of them and neighbours to the right of them, indeed almost everyone in Newton, Hatherton, Houghton, Foxton, Longston and Shorestone Avenues, had extensions built and acquired spacious, attractive, modern kitchens. Not my parents. I don't think my father would have made a stand against it, but my mother would not countenance the acceptance of the money. To her, this would have made her home into some kind of hybrid council house, and herself into a person who had accepted charity. Either that, or she knew they could not afford the other half of the cost, and she preferred to take a principled stance rather than to admit it. Sadly, it caused a slight rift in one of their few genuine friendships of long standing. Ross and Florence, who took them to the Round Table Dance, had come to live a few doors away not long before. They did take the money, made an impressive change to the back of their house, and plainly were offended by the superior attitude taken by my mother.

Anyway, she was the one to suffer, continuing as she did in her unimproved kitchen. This was a space about seven feet square. Along the back wall under the window was a marble topped cupboard; a large pot sink (of exactly the type fashionable again now), was in the corner. In the opposite wall a door opened into the space under the top of the stairs, fitted with shelves as the pantry. That was it. The gas cooker was outside the kitchen in a gloomy area at the back of the adjoining garage. In part, this was because there had to be space, even in this tiny kitchen, for my mother to deal with some ladies who came to have their hair done. She was a skilful hair-dresser, and when she gave up 'the shop' there were a few of her clients who would not go to anyone else. One or two stayed with her for a further twenty years.

If there is here no mention of fridges and washing machines, this is because for a long time we did not have any. A fridge was, of course, less of a necessity in households where it was taken for granted that the wife would shop every day, where she would take her order book into the Co-op twice a week and groceries would be brought by a boy on a bicycle with a huge basket on the front. Milk arrived daily on the doorstep, brought on a rattling cart pulled by a grey horse with huge hairy hooves. In winter, the milk was often frozen, and its expansion in the bottle had pushed a plug of stiffened cream up, with the silver cap sitting on it like a hat. I loved this, surreptitiously eating the frozen cream as I carried the bottles to the kitchen. In summer, the milk bottles were put into a bucket of water in the bottom of the pantry, in the often vain hope that it would stay fresh. When the milk cart came, I liked to sit on the kerb when the horse trudged along, to look up into the rheumy brown eyes inside the blinkers he wore. He clicked and shifted his hooves, and set off again with a jerk and rattle as soon as he heard the milkman put down the bottles. This meant the man was driven by the rhythm of the horse, scuttling from house to house, grabbing from the metal crates in the brief period that the horse stood still. I was rather embarrassed by the fact that if my father was at home he would watch from the window, and if the horse deposited a pile of steaming straw-filled droppings in the length of road outside our garden, out he would come with a shovel and bucket, and take it into the garage to rot down until it was ready to put on the roses.

So, no fridge, and no washing machine. Washing day, Monday of course, was hateful, winter and summer alike, but worse in winter. All the beds were stripped, almost before we could get out of them, and big pans were put on the cooker to boil water. One old grey pan was used exclusively for boiling hankies, which had to bubble for quite a while to ensure the removal of all dirt and stains. The rest of the hot water went in, load after load, to the receptacle known in the North East as the poss tub. This was a metal container big enough to hold two or three sheets at a time. The soap for the process was hard work for me. This was because the new soap, which was a big yellow block, from the Co-op, had to be grated. This was my finger-skinning job, even when I was only four or five. When a panful was prepared, it was mixed with water, then slowly melted on the cooker, turning into a thickly viscous slime. This would last for two or three washing days; the slime cooled into a loose greyish jelly that could be ladled into the hot water as needed. Slopping some of this out of the pan into the poss tub turned my stomach. It put me in mind of some kind of vile bodily excretion, possibly the phlegm of the goblins who lived in a cave near our beach. These were stunted warty creatures, clawed like crabs, stinking like old seaweed. They lived on rotting fish and killed children by biting out their guts. Or so I had been told in secret whispers by other, older, children.

Once the tub and its contents were ready, the process of possing began. The implement, the poss stick, resembled nothing so much as a copper warming pan on the end of a thick broom handle. The copper part at the end was a hollow dome with holes around the edge, which, when pushed up and down, forced the hot soapy water to bubble through the fabric of the bedding. Sheets, pillowcases, towels, shirts went through this process. Often I was expected to wield the poss stick for a while. It was impossibly hard work, leaving me limp and shaking after only a few minutes.

The remainder of the laundry, our underclothes, socks and stockings, was washed by hand in the sink. Then everything had to be mangled. Our mangle, an old one, had a pair of wooden rollers (more modern ones were rubber), turned against each other by a handle, between which the washing was forced, in order to have the water squeezed out of it. To avoid splashing all over the floor, the clothing was wrung out by hand between the tub and the mangle, a process which I was expected to share, and which tore the skin from the sides of my nails after a while. All our mangling was done into another big tub filled with clean water for rinsing, then it was mangled again before being hung out to dry. Several years later, when my mother acquired the only electric washing machine she ever owned, it consisted of a tub in which electricity turned a paddle to agitate the laundry, replacing the poss stick, and electricity turned a mangle. In our house all this took place in the gloomy space at the back of the garage that passed as part of our kitchen.

When I say the washing was hung out to dry, I mean it was put somewhere dependent on the weather. If it was fine, then it did hang on the washing line in the back garden. Wet Mondays in winter were the worst days imaginable to me. Around the dining room fire would be placed the clothes horse, an object like two wooden gates held together with hinges made of fabric webbing, and on it was hung the wet bedlinen. This meant that even this room was cold, and what is more, filled with the damp miasma of steaming sheets. For as long as I could get away with it, I would creep between the washing and the fire, where it was warm but wet. Of course, having a little child huddled within inches of an unprotected open fire is not advisable, so my refuge would be quickly invaded, and I was firmly dragged out, probably to be smacked.

Smacking was practised with some frequency, but I think our household was very much like most others of the time. 'Spare the rod and spoil the child' was still a belief. Even our mild-mannered father subscribed to this notion. I can remember, although my brother does not, that once, when a ball broke a pane of the greenhouse, Kit was briskly given a couple of strokes on the bottom with a garden cane. A quick one delivered with justice, I did not like, but also did not resent. But my mother had a sudden and vicious temper sometimes, and the punishment would arise from her loss of control rather than as a response to the wrongdoing. One hot summer day, when I was perhaps seven years old, I was sent to buy a family-size block of ice cream from a shop about five or six minutes walk away from home. I held it in my hands carefully on the return journey; the shopkeeper had not given me a paper bag. Very quickly the ice cream began to melt, and as it dripped I licked it off my hands. Truly, I was not deliberately eating it, but by the time I got home, the whole block was soft, distorted in shape, and diminished in size. My mother opened the cardboard wrapping, and without a word smacked the dripping remains straight into my face. The shock and loss of dignity were all the greater because we were not alone; one of the hairdressing clients was in the kitchen at the time. I believe she was as abashed as I was.

If washing day was bad, baking day was lovely. My mother did not need to do a great deal of baking; she brought Grandma's cakes home with her every Sunday, and her occasional attempts at bread were more because she enjoyed doing it, than from necessity. But she made excellent biscuits. I loved to help, squashing sugar and butter together, dolloping golden syrup off a warmed spoon, and cutting the dough with little metal cutters the shape of gingerbread men or the initial letters of our names. Some had chopped nuts sprinkled on top, some half a glace cherry pushed onto them. There was always a bowl to clean out and lick afterwards.

I also enjoyed making drop scones, a thick pancake mixture cooked on a black iron plate. These were very quick to make, and appeared on the tea table still warm and ready for melting butter. The iron pan was called a girdle in those parts, rather than a griddle, and the same mixture with the addition of sultanas and a little baking powder made girdle scones.

We made sweets too, toffee and fudge. These were dangerous because the sugar had to cook at such a high temperature, but, closely watched, I made my own. I loved the moment of testing the toffee by dripping it into cold water and finding it went hard, or even better, stayed slightly soft and chewy. One amazing time, we tried making cinder toffee by adding bicarbonate of soda to the hot toffee, and watching it surge up the pan like yellow lava trying to erupt. Sad little children of nowadays who only ever taste this as the unadventurous insides of a Crunchie bar!

Eating was a significant part of our lives. As with most of her activities, my mother did not believe she cooked well, but she was wrong. I think she made the mistake of thinking that because she could not afford elaborate or expensive ingredients, the results of her work were second rate. In fact, we ate very well; simple homely meals that nowadays are admired and served in restaurants.

Every morning we had cooked breakfast, the whole family sitting down to the table, with linen napkins and napkin rings! Often we began with porridge, then there were always eggs, boiled or fried with bacon or poached or scrambled. I liked boiled eggs best, scooped out of the shell into a cup, chopped up and spread on toast. We had our main meal at mid-day, again all four of us. My brother and I came home from school; school dinners were another of those almost charitable offerings that people in council houses may need, but not us. In retrospect, I realise that again my mother was hiding behind an invented principle. School dinners were a shilling, ten shillings a week for the two of us. She could certainly feed us better at home for less, but pride would never allow her to admit these financial restrictions. She was, however, fine at saying we could not afford luxuries; there was a virtuous restraint in this.

The pattern of the week's dinners began with Sunday. Brisket of beef was quite cheap, and pot-roasted slowly it became meltingly tender and made delicious gravy. Roast or mashed potatoes, carrots, peas and Yorkshire pudding, followed by a steamed pudding and custard, was the usual sort of offering. The piece of beef was large, so it made shepherd's pie on Monday and rissoles on Tuesday. Except for tinned peas in winter, all our vegetables were fresh and seasonal. The gravy from the brisket was excellent with a mixture of mashed potatoes and swede. As an alternative we would have a shoulder of lamb, cheaper than leg, but just as good served with home-made mint sauce, the mint picked from the garden.

We had fish on Wednesday and Friday, twice a week because this was economical for a family living beside the sea in a fishing village. Remembering the fishing industry in Cullercoats recalls a lost time. It was receding then, in some ways for the good. On Front Street, leading down to the sea, was a row of impossibly picturesque cottages, white-walled with sagging dark slate roofs, leaning on each other as if for support against the Arctic gales that surged in over the cliffs. Here the fisher families still lived, in two rooms without much in the way of sanitation. I was shocked when the cottages were suddenly demolished in the mid sixties, but I could never have lived in one. The fishing was done in large high-prowed rowing boats called cobles, their curved shape and clinker construction showing their Viking ancestry. It was rare for one to have an engine. The men stood in them to row strongly and rhythmically with long oars out into the slow white-capped swell of the North Sea. They fished with nets, and with crab and lobster pots, which were actually baskets made of rope on a curved wooden frame. The pots were thrown into the waves, their positions marked by little pointed flags that fluttered on the surface.

The fish was sold from tables outside the cottage doors. We went to Taylor's cottage because my mother had been at school with Mrs. Taylor, and her daughter Margaret was in my Brownie pack. Skate was my favourite, cooked in butter, with a slice of lemon. Cod is usually a deep sea fish, but the men caught it anyway, by rowing two or three miles out on calm nights, so it was a bit more expensive, but not such a luxury that we could not have it. All the fish cost just pence on that shore, including crabs and even lobster, but these were sold live and required a degree of courage to handle and cook them, so they remained off our menu. My mother baked the cod, in a way that I have since seen only in Southern Spain and Italy, that is, by covering it completely with a thick layer of salt, which retained its moisture, and lightly flavoured the fish. Another favourite I knew only as 'flatfish', some kind of plaice or sole, I guess. This was fried in dripping so that its finny edges became crisp. Partly cooked small wedges of potato mixed with finely chopped onion were browned in the pan beside the fish. In those days, nobody called these sauté potatoes, but I recognised them years later, when exposed to a more sophisticated cuisine.

Saturday's midday meal was more casual, I don't recall why. We had fried egg and chips and fried mushrooms. Presumably we did not have breakfast eggs on that day, but I don't remember.

That leaves Thursday, sometimes not such a good day. There was a shop in Whitley Bay called the Tripe Shop. Imagine! A shop devoted to the sale of nothing but tripes. Actually, they also sold pig's trotters and something horrible called cowheel, but we never had to resort to these. Tripe, however, was apparently a useful standby if funds were running low. In the shop the tripes were displayed on large trays, piles of white and beige crumpled sheets, their convoluted surfaces like fine rubbery doormats. That is pretty much

The Tyne Commissioner's yacht

The crew of the yacht

Me aged about six

My great grandparents, grandmother,
great aunts, great uncle

Me and my brother Kit

Me and Maureen my first friend

Mrs Pascoe's dancing school, me top right

Cullercoats Swimming Club

Swimming Club Gala at Hawkey's Lane,
men's obstacle race

Grandma, Mrs Crow, Auntie Lizzie, Dad,
Uncle Willie, me and Kit

My parents and me

My parents on their wedding day,
Feb 4th 1942

The canoe Mishe Nahma, me at the stern,
Sandra in front, her sister inside

what they felt like when cooked, though I must say I did not become expert in the merits of various tripes, by dint of refusing to eat it. I did not go hungry however, as I enjoyed the white sauce with onions and the mashed potato that went with it.

Although this in my memory seemed to represent the typical pattern, the weekly menu also included quite a wide range of other comfortable meals. My mother made an excellent steak and kidney pudding, succulent meat, gravy and mushrooms steamed in a suet crust; or the same mixture would appear as a pie with delicate pastry. Unusually for a child, I loved liver, soft and tender with its accompaniment of crispy fried onions and dark gravy with buttery mashed potatoes. Another delicious offering my mother called Irish stew. This was mutton (not lamb) boiled with potatoes, carrots and onions, a rather bland mixture made exceptional by serving it with tomato ketchup. There were rotund brown sausages, lamb chops with crisp brown fatty edges, pork ribs slowly baked in a sauce of vinegar, sugar and home-made tomato chutney, so that the meat fell from the bones.

Puddings were as good. My mother performed the whole repertoire of steamed pudding; spotted dick, jam roly-poly, syrup dumpling. There were succulent fruit pies and crumbles, nothing exotic, just apple, rhubarb, black-berry, gooseberry. A Sunday favourite had Bramley apple baked beneath soft buttery sponge. Which reminds me of baked apples, huge ones with the cores scooped out and a big spoonful of mincemeat in the middle. Who nowadays makes rice pudding; one tablespoon of pudding rice to one pint of Jersey milk, with one tablespoon of sugar and a good sprinkling of freshly ground nutmeg on top, baked slowly, slowly, so the rice and the milk melted together, and a chewy toffee flavoured brown skin formed on top?

Because of the dinner in the middle of the day (I never understood what was meant by the word 'lunch'), our evening meal, which was finished before six o'clock, was referred to as tea. More cooking was required; toasted cheese, pease pudding so voluptuous and tasty, various soups with dumplings cooked in them, flan – same thing is now known as quiche. Ham for sandwiches came from another specialist shop in Whitley Bay, the Pork Shop. Here the parts of a pig that provided various meats were obvious, so I knew that ham came from close to a pig's bottom. I did not like it much, not because of its anatomical origin, but because it was rather dry and very salty. Grandma prepared hams herself, and hers were sweeter and moister. Still it was better than chaps and chitterlings, ears, or even a whole head boiled and served with pickles. These I saw for sale in the Pork Shop, but never could imagine eating. I averted my eyes from the ox tongues complete all the way back to the choky bit out of the throat, because I did not want to stop enjoying the delicate pink meat that we ate with lettuce and cucumber.

There was a feature of shopping in those days, which has, as far as I can see, completely disappeared. It arose from the fact that hardly anything was pre-packed, so shopkeepers would find that they had leftovers and broken bits that could be sold off cheaply. Broken biscuits were the commonest; a big bag of mixed bits would be a few pence. I also remember mixed bags of sweets (the remains from the bottoms of the jars), ham bones, which made good stock for split pea soup, and stale bread that could be made into crumbs for sage and onion stuffing. In spite of her stand against the receipt of charity and its implication of poverty, my mother would buy these things (except the biscuits, as she made her own), because mostly they represented an opportunity to produce something worthwhile with a bit of virtuous effort.

Actually, it seems to me looking back that shopkeepers were prepared, and allowed, to sell almost anything if it made a few pennies. After Brownies, my friend Sandra and I would go to the fish and chip shop to buy two penn'orth of batter. This was a bagful of the crumbs of batter that had drifted off the fish during the frying process. It was skimmed out of the fat and collected in a golden crispy pile, to provide a very tasty but thoroughly indigestible snack.

The worst exploitation of customers I remember, however, occurred in the sweet shop that was on our route to school. Today, it would be shut down under some public health law; then, I can't say we liked it, but needs must when it was the only place available to us without taking a detour which would have made us late. It was a corner shop on Station Road run by a middle-aged couple who would have been well cast in a Dracula movie. The husband was short and sinister, wearing a food-stained dark suit, his black hair greased to his head, and his face a patchwork of unshaven tufts. His wild-haired wife, who walked with a strange sideways gait, one foot turned almost at right angles to the other, did most of the serving in the shop. She used old newspaper to wrap the sweets, which meant that her hands were black. Roald Dahl describes a very similar character in his book 'Boy', so maybe such a person was a common phenomenon. They had a disabled son, John, who did not go to school anywhere. He spent most of his time at the window of the flat above the shop, big knobbed hands pressed to the glass like distorted starfish, his overlarge head bobbing on his thin neck. He must have been sixteen or so when I was going to the Juniors as a seven-year-old, and his parents decided he needed an occupation. So they set him to making toffee, which they would sell in the shop. Invariably it was burned, almost black and so brittle it would cut your mouth, and for some reason often had dead ants embedded in it. However, it was cheap so we bought it. The sense of getting a bargain overcame our disgust at its taste and texture. Also, I think we realised that horrible as it may have been, John had achieved something in its production and it would have been unkind of us to reject it.

Household shopping with my mother I enjoyed, although it cannot always have been much fun for her. Although an order from the Co-op was delivered each week, she still had quite a burden to carry in her big red tartan shopping bag. We walked to the shops on Whitley Road, a round trip of about a mile and a half. When my brother was very small I walked holding the handle of his pram, a big black affair like the bottom half of a miniature coach. The shopping must have been easier then, as the pram was amply big enough to contain one normal-sized baby and provisions for the rest of the family for a week. Its size and usefulness makes it all the more remarkable that on one occasion, my mother left it, and him, outside Woolworths, and got all the way home before she remembered. Her panic, and the memory of her sprinting off along the street to reclaim him, fills me with retrospective pity. At the time, I too was upset, because I thought he was probably crying for us and had no one to cuddle him. It must have been at that time when her mind was on the ill health of her father, and she was accustomed to doing her errands in a hurry while I was left at home with him and the grandfather-sitter. Also, there seemed to have been a stronger sense of collective caring, so babies in prams could be left outside shops. Perception or reality? Was it a safer world, or were the prams just too big? Anyway, little Kit (or Kirton as he was at that time) came home happy and smiling.

As well as feeding us and keeping us reasonably clean, my mother clothed us largely by her own efforts. Evenings, with the radio for entertainment, she would be knitting, and many afternoons, especially in winter, were spent working the Singer sewing machine. This was a beautiful thing, with its shapely body of black lacquered metal, its ornate curvaceous gold lettering, and the swinging rhythm of its movement. It was quite a modern one, with a handle to turn, rather than the metal treadle of a previous generation. I would sit alongside my mother, and turn the handle for her, so that her hands were free to guide the fabric. Of course, she did not need this, being even more speedy and skilful without my help.

Except for a woollen waistcoat now and then, she did not make clothes for my father. His unvarying uniform of suit, shirt and tie, or sports jacket, flannels, shirt and tie, did not lend itself to making at home. But she turned out almost every garment worn by herself, my brother and me. This went on until we were of an age to demand bought clothes, fashionable but of inferior quality. Throughout my young childhood, I wore a series of outfits of such similarity as to be virtually a uniform. In winter, on weekdays and Saturdays, it was a pleated skirt and a knitted twinset. The pleated skirts I liked best were tartan kilts, complete with fringed edge to the fabric, and a big pin to hold the flap. The twinset, for warmth had long sleeves for both jumper and cardigan. They were colourful outfits, the woollens matching the red or yellow or blue of the tartan. The most special woollies were Fair Isle, lovely intricate coloured patterns on a background of cream or fawn. On Sundays, I always, until about the age of twelve, had a dark red wool dress with a white lace collar. Our coats were not home made, but we wore them with a range of knitted gloves, scarves and hats. My favourite hats were round berets with a circular Fair Isle pattern.

In summer, the range was more varied, but always dresses. These were usually flowered cotton or checked gingham, but I had a few best frocks that were fine needlecord, velvet or silk. A favourite one was pink figured silk, with Bo-beep pockets. These were round, and gathered onto the dress like little pouches. The clarity of this memory lies in an unpleasant adventure I had while wearing it. My Grandma and I walked up the lonnen (a grassy lane) from The Crest to Mr. Elwyn's farm, a walk we often enjoyed on a Sunday afternoon. On this occasion we went into the byre to watch the milking, and I stood too close to the back end of a cow. A pink silk dress with pockets artfully designed to stand slightly open does not recover well from being doused in fresh and very wet manure.

My brother also wore hand-made clothes, simply grey shorts and a series of jumpers, not so colourful as he was a boy. He had a little suit, with short trousers, for Sundays. His clothing adventure involved a knitted swim-suit, knickers with a bib and straps, which looked really cute until he ran into the sea. The water weighed down the wool such that when he turned round to come out, the straps stretched down to his ankles, and he waddled from the waves naked, with his swimsuit dragging round his feet. Fortunately he was only three when this happened.

When I remember those childhood days, one set of memories that invokes security and calm is of time spent sitting in the corner of the kitchen while my mother dealt with her hairdressing clients. She spent just one after-noon, and sometimes part of an evening, each week, with these women who were not quite friends, much more than acquaintances. Apart from a couple of them who were also members of the Swimming Club, my mother never spent time with them outside of her own kitchen. But the relationships had the intimacy born of very long conversations; years long, topics started, paused, picked up a week later. They ranged over the trivial details of bread and bunions, recipes and relations. Sometimes the talk would be more significant, about quarrels and disasters, whether the new false teeth suited, or the daughter's fiancé.

I had a little square stool with a woven seagrass top. As soon as I heard the knock at the door, I would hurry to pull this out from its place under the sideboard, so that I would be quiet and unobtrusive in my corner as the lady came in. This had the comfort of familiarity for me, as I must have been doing it since babyhood, when my mother still had 'the shop'.

I suppose the conversations I eavesdropped were reflective of family life, the births marriages and deaths department. Most of the stories I remember, however, were about illness. It seems a paradox that I recall the time with pleasure and a feeling of security, although the subject matter was so often grim and frightening. There was someone's neighbour with a growth in his throat that slowly choked him to death. There was the case of an operation for impacted wisdom teeth during which the patient woke up. People's insides burst, their eyes turned yellow, their toes were cut off. I became very scared of haemorrhoids, especially as I knew they were the result of sitting on the cold pavement, something I had done frequently. As for childbirth, it was impossible to imagine anything worse than the hours of screaming agony involved. Why did women have babies, especially more than once? It could only be because it happened unexpectedly and unavoidably as a result of being female. I tried to express my disquiet to my mother, only to be told that when you had your baby in your arms you forgot the pain. This was clearly a lie; time after time I heard these women in our kitchen describing their pain pretty accurately, so I was left confused as well as nervous.

Nevertheless, I loved to sit in that corner and listen. All the other stories, about their children, their neighbours, their homes, gave me a sense of the kindliness of women. I could feel in their soft, low voices their reliability, their motherliness. Also, the stories were serial; we would have weeks of preparation for a daughter's wedding, followed by pieces of cake and black and white photographs. There were plans for holidays, and then descriptions of Scarborough or Torquay or Clacton. I saw the pride and anxiety felt for children, their own and other people's. Joan from along the street, who gained a State Scholarship for university, in spite of being badly crippled by polio. Mrs. Hopper's son, Reggie, for whom school had been a struggle, got a job as the mayor's chauffeur.

Sometimes, I didn't understand the stories as clearly as I sensed the emotional response. A handsome, clever boy from the next street went off to university in London. His widowed mother was so proud. Then one of my mother's clients came with the news that the boy had been arrested for doing something bad in a station toilet. I couldn't guess from the conversation what he had done, but I felt the shock and the sympathy for the woman whose beautiful son had wounded her beyond bearing.

All the time, I was a small, silent, unregarded presence, absorbing as much information as I could about the lives of adults. Only once, as I sat quietly listening, was there a pause, a slight gesture to my mother, and she sent me off out of the room to do something elsewhere. I felt offended, although by what I didn't know. It never occurred to me that I was hearing secrets.

My mother's ministrations to these women involved the use of equipment that would now be found only in a museum. Most of the customers had a shampoo and set. The wet hair was carefully combed and pinched into a series of parallel waves, each of which was then held in place by pairs of metal combs joined by a spring. Then the ends of the hair were twisted into tiny flat spiral curls, secured by Kirby grips. The whole lot was covered by a hair net, and the customer sat for half an hour under the hood of the hairdryer. Hand dryers such as we have today were available, but regarded by my mother as hopelessly amateur. While drying, the lady would drink tea and eat our home made biscuits.

A few ladies, whose hair was longer, had Marcel waves. The equipment for this was a pair of metal tongs heated on a small burner, which glowed with the pretty purple flame of methylated spirits. The hot tongs gripped the hair, making grooved waves as my mother's skilled hands turned them. I loved the regular rhythm of the movement, the warm smell of the burning spirits and the hot clean hair. Mrs. Ellender, who was nearly eighty for years of my childhood, nevertheless had lovely brown hair two feet long. This was waved exquisitely from scalp to tip, then twisted into two perfect coils on the nape of her neck, where it stayed until a week later, when she would return for the process to be repeated.

The most expensive and time-consuming operation was a perm. This used both chemicals and heat. The perm machine was a heavy black frame around a set of vertical metal rods, heated by electricity. Onto these rods were gripped the perm curlers, each one like a little fingerless hand with a black Bakelite handle. First the hair was washed, then strand after strand was soaked in a chemical liquid, wrapped in a piece of tissue paper, and wound round a thin metal roller. Then the hot curler was clamped onto the roller. To avoid burning the scalp (and this was not a wholly reliable method), a piece of foam rubber was tucked under each one. By the time this part of the operation was complete, about thirty heavy lumps of hot metal were hanging on the victim's head. I know how uncomfortable it was because the process was done to me on several occasions, one aspect of my plainness being straight hair. Once the curlers were cold, they could be removed, the hair was shampooed again, then set in the usual way. It was not an enjoyable experience, but the resulting curls were glossy, apparently natural, and lasted until the hair grew out.

These, then, were my days. Once I had started going to school, I must have missed many of the conversations in the kitchen, except in the holidays, when I willingly slipped back into that quiet routine. One by one, the ladies disappeared. Did they die? Did they get too old to need hairdos? One or two moved away, to places like Rothbury or Corbridge, lovely places in the countryside, when their husbands retired. But, even when I went away to university there were still two, still having their Marcel waves and pin curls and cups of tea on Thursday afternoons.

The
Swimming
Club

I think of that coast as so beautiful and so fierce. The northern beaches of Northumberland, the endless gleaming plains of sand, the constant rolling waves, with the brooding romantic dark silhouettes of castles at Bamburgh and Dunstanburgh, are famous. They are filmstar landscapes, locations on which gaudily accoutred horses have galloped with artfully flying manes and tails, ridden by mediaeval priests and kings, Peter O'Toole and Richard Burton.

When the film crews are absent, the great beaches of the North are virtually empty. On a fine day, the wide flat pools left by the tide reflect the moving sky, the sea is navy blue and emerald green, and flicks a rippled edge at the shore. In the distant waves the improbable jagged mound of Lindisfarne, the Holy Island, floats mistily, a hazy and ghostly reminder of the endless history of the place. Also a reminder that its peaceful aspect is always an illusion to be shattered by violence. As a child at school I loved and feared the Viking stories, of 'the heathen (who) miserably destroyed God's church in Lindisfarne by rapine and slaughter.' More often the violence is of nature, this being the coast of Grace Darling, held up to us as a model of courage, and one possible to emulate, because she too was a Northumberland girl. The power and rage of the sea was all too obvious; also clear was the knowledge that if you found yourself alone in a small boat in a raging storm near a shipwreck, you would follow her example and row to the rescue.

The southern end of the Northumberland coast (the district name Tyne and Wear did not exist until after I left the county), is smaller in scale, and populous, the seaward boundary of the Newcastle conurbation. A rather strange and contrary thing has happened to the busy-ness of those beaches, however. When I was young, the conurbation was smaller, the villages and small towns were more separate with substantial bits of countryside between. But the beaches of Whitley Bay, Cullercoats and Tynemouth were popular, even crowded on fine summer days. Now, although the local population has grown, and hardly a field or wood is left between Tynemouth Priory and the centre of Newcastle, the beaches are often empty, save for a lone dog walker, or a few families having a day out behind their plastic windbreaks. Everyone prefers to be in Tenerife or Majorca or the Maldives. Even the Swimming Club has gone.

The bay at Cullercoats is a piece of topographical perfection. To the north it is divided by half a mile of tumbled rockiness from the stretch of pale sand that serves the erstwhile resort of Whitley Bay. To the south, beyond a hump-backed headland that juts out into another area of rocks, is the yellower expanse of Tynemouth Long Sands. Between these rocky jaws, the sea slips easily in over smooth sand to the harbour of Cullercoats. The natural shape is of a double bay, two curved beaches of soft clean sand facing each other, with a jut of cliff between them. To enhance this gentle shape, a massive stone breakwater or pier has been built out from each side to enclose the harbour even more securely. I don't know how old these great walls are. Built of wave-softened yellow sandstone, they look truly ancient. At high tide, the bay fills like a cup, leaving a warm sliver of sand on each side, called North Beach and South Beach. At low tide, the water recedes, until just the ends of the piers stand with their feet in the water. Sometimes, at spring tides, the beaches can be wholly covered, then at low tide the sea leaves the stone foundations bare, showing an expanse of glistening brown straps of weed where normally there is sea.

Living there, about a quarter of a mile from the sea front, it was impossible to be unaware of the moods of the sea. Only on the finest and calmest of days was it silent. These were days of the clear light reflected from water as pale as the sky, both winter and summer, when the whole view from the cliff top was coloured blue and white and gold. Stormy days could happen at any time of the year, and often the storm would be of the sea and not of the land. Under a clear sky, the sea would rise, rolling to the shore in iron grey parallel undulations, each wave galloping up to crash and spread and draw back under the skirts of the next. At Cullercoats the cliffs are about forty feet high, but often the power of the storm would drive the sea so hard against the land that great clouds of white spray would crash up over the cliff top, wetting the pavement and any children who enjoyed standing in the path of the onslaught.

The sinister times were quiet winter nights, when banks of fog rolled over the water, reaching grey fingers into the streets and gardens, and filling the darkness outside my bedroom window. Always slow to sleep, I would lie listening to the blanketed silence, broken regularly by the sepulchral howl of the foghorns at the mouth of the Tyne and further away at the Souter Lighthouse. These creatures moaned their sonorous calls into the darkness, distant but insistent, so that even my chilly bedroom seemed snug and safe.

Around the shoreline of the bay were several significant buildings. On the cliff top above North Beach was the Watch House, more or less redundant by the time I knew it, but from which generations of coast guards had kept a physical vigil over the movement of the sea. Below this, at the back of the beach, was the lifeboat house, containing the beautiful blue and white boat, which from time to time was called out by rockets that cracked over the rooftops. Everyone who heard them, crew or not, ran to the beach in response. The launching of the boat was a rather arduous process. The slipway ran down, not into the water but onto the sand, so even at high tide a tractor was needed to pull the boat into the water. Once launched, it bounced and battered its way out over the waves to retrieve some luckless fisherman or yachtsman. I remember the inauguration of this boat. The great importance of the event was marked by the fact that we had an hour or so out of school, walking in crocodile the hundred yards or so, to range ourselves along the path that led down to the beach. There was quite a long wait, lightened by scuffing gravel down onto the heads of the phalanx on the stretch of the path below us. Their teacher, Mrs. Cross, who was well named, kept looking up with an expression that said we were unaware of the significance of this important occasion for our village. Then, for a few moments it felt exciting as the boat was rolled several yards out of its house, christened, then rolled in again.

Also on North Beach was the Aquarium. It cost money to go in there, and it contained in tanks the very shrimps, crabs, fish and sea anemones that we could find for nothing in the rock pools, so it was visited rarely. Now I believe it is an important department of Newcastle University with marine biologists doing interesting research. Perhaps that was the case then too.

On South Beach the only building was the Swimming Club. It stood rather grandly against the base of the cliff at the root of the south pier, thus having a view into the bay and out to sea. A wooden building, painted dark green, and two storeys high, it was attached to massive concrete posts underneath, and had its back firmly anchored into the face of the cliff. The lower storey contained the ladies' changing room. Upstairs was the men's changing room, and a large area called the verandah. This had windows on the three outward-facing sides, and was furnished with wooden tables and chairs, a sink and an urn to boil water for the tea, a very important implement. There were perhaps a hundred members, including children, of whom thirty or forty formed the core, a selection of whom could be relied upon to be present almost any day of the year. My mother, my brother and I were amongst these.

In spite of my awareness of the changing power of the sea, I never felt that it was dangerous to me. Familiarity had given me an almost instinctive knowledge of when it was welcoming and when it was not, so that I would not put myself in danger. We, the children of the Swimming Club, were allowed a degree of freedom on that shore that surprises me when I recall it. From early Spring to late Autumn the beach and the clubhouse were an extension of our homes; most days, we did not go home from school, but down to the beach. This was about three minutes brisk trot, so we would be there with almost half an afternoon of sunshine and playtime. The sun did shine, although it was not always warm, and our mothers would be sitting in their big half circle of deck chairs, waiting for the cascade of children ready for tea and orange squash and tomato sandwiches. The children were Pam and Jeff, Christine and Paul, Christine and Barbara, John, Tom, Topsy, June, Sandra, Kit, me, others whose names I have forgotten, but whose faces are as fresh and bright in my memory as ever they were in life. Friendships between individuals were formed, forgotten and formed again. Pam was in my class at school, so sometimes we gravitated together, sometimes she went off with Sandra who was her cousin. Kit and Jeff were friends; almost fifty years later, they still are.

Some of those children I remember for particular experiences. Sandra Rose looked as pretty and demure as her name, but she was the one who got a stick and with it squashed the corpse of a rat until its coiled guts popped out. The rest of us squatted in a circle to watch with heaving stomachs, but she calmly pointed out how interesting it was. I think she was probably six at the time. Tom said he would teach me to sail, then showed off so dramatically with his small dinghy in a stiff breeze that I was terrified. We got several hundred yards out to sea, when there was a slight impact as the boat ran over perhaps a piece of floating wood. Tom expertly hove to and suggested that I slip overboard to inspect for damage. I was obedient, so I slid gingerly into the water, and pulled myself hand over hand around the hull looking for non-existent holes. Only when I had completed my inspection did I realise he was laughing.

Much of our activity on and around the water was tolerated by the adults, on the assumption that we were all strong swimmers. Learning to swim in the North Sea at an early age makes or breaks you as a swimmer, I suppose, but I remember all of those children as competent and fearless in the water. My own first moments of swimming at the age of four I recall with an echo of the exhilaration of the time. It happened unexpectedly, when I was playing in the soft waves that would roll into the bay on breezy summer days. The game was to bounce out through the waves until the water was chest high, then turn and throw yourself forwards so the force of the wave carried you the few yards onto the beach. I got better and better at keeping my feet up so that I achieved quite a long glide before my stomach scraped over the sand. Then I mistimed my jump, the wave ran ahead of me and I was off the bottom in the deeper water behind it. I paddled rapidly with hands and feet and suddenly realised the freedom of flying in the water. All my limbs were lithe and moving, my body was light. I wanted to scream and jump and dance with excitement, but more, I wanted to do it again. Time after time I scrambled back into the water deep enough to float me, to fly again with frantic arms and legs, until I was exhausted, blue and juddering with cold.

Kit and I had a small boat of our own, a two seater kayak with double ended paddles. Our father built it using instructions sent from PGL, who now run adventure holidays for children. Dad made an excellent job of it, although I doubt whether he realised when he began just how complex a task it would be. The boat had a wooden frame, a series of plywood panels jigsawed into a cross-section shape then pierced with many large carefully cut holes to make them light. These were held together laterally with curved struts, made into that shape by bending strips of wood into shape, bracing them with hemp string, and soaking them in the bath for days on end. Once the wooden frame was completed it was covered with thick canvas, water-proofed with many coats of linseed oil. At least Kit and I could help with this part of the construction, in the process becoming so impregnated with the oil that the smell of cricket bats hovered around us for days. We painted it red and white, and named it Mishe Nahma after the sturgeon in the poem of Hiawatha, which I was reading at the time.

We pushed it down to the sea on a trolley, also specially constructed. It was beautiful, and strong, and survived all of my childhood, and Kit's, eventually being sold to some more children when Kit was fifteen and worked a summer holiday for a local boat builder who gave him a new one in payment. One of the unwritten safety rules of the beach applied to the use of the canoe; this was that we were not allowed to go beyond the piers. Most of the time we were content to comply with this instruction, because, with the tide in, there was a large area of water in which to paddle about. We could fish with crab lines out in the middle of the bay, although always the little brown-backed crabs were unhooked and tossed back. Usually the water was so clear that the sandy bottom was visible twenty feet below, and quietly rocking on the surface, we could watch the silent fish glide beneath us.

Sometimes, if my mother was not in the clubhouse to see what I was doing, and the sea was calm, I would venture beyond the piers into the open sea, never quite far enough to see beyond the headlands onto both of the long beaches of Whitley Bay and Tynemouth, but giving myself a wide view of Cullercoats, the enclosing arms of the bay, the tall Georgian houses along the cliff top, the graceful steeple of St. George's church. I could sit out beyond the middle of the bay, and see that on the cliff between the twin beaches a tall beacon stood. Behind it, the row of three storey houses of Beverley Terrace was broken. One low house, Beacon House, crouched down so that the other beacon was visible behind it. When the two were aligned in your view from the sea, you could head for harbour knowing that the rocks were safely at a distance on each side of you. Both masts carried a light, and I imagined how it must be for the fishermen returning in the sea-blackness of night, rowing in and turning towards those two glowing points, heaving the oars until the two became one, and the harbour was ahead.

During our seaside days we children played and explored on the shore as well as the water. When the tide was low, an area of rocks and pools was exposed on the seaward side of the piers. With much practice and familiarity, we acquired a rapid but cautious gait that enabled us to run about on the weedy rocks without falling, and could jump from rock to rock where the yellow stone was covered with barnacles. We gave unimaginative names to the features of this landscape. A long fissure between taller rocks, where the water dragged the tendrils of a blood coloured weed, we called the Red River. A flat raised island of rock, detached from the shore at all but the lowest tide, was the Crab's Back, or the Bear's Back. Beneath the headland that divided our home territory from Tynemouth Long Sands was the Fairy Cave, a scoop only a few yards deep into the bottom of the cliff face, but where you could enter in Cullercoats and exit in Tynemouth. This was where I had been told by older children that the gut-chewing goblins lived. I never believed it, but passed on the story to the younger ones anyway.

Our pastimes in this watery world consisted mostly in finding and interfering with its natural inhabitants. The deep red sea anemones, stuck to the rocks like sucked cough sweets, we believed to be seriously poisonous. Under water they spread their flowery tentacles. Over and over we would touch these with sticks or strands of weed, and watch them clench like small hands over the illusion of prey. I imagined that if you were unwary enough to stick a finger in there, it would come out shrunken and sucked empty of blood. We called the creatures bloodsuckers.

My favourites were hermit crabs. They took over the empty shells of winkles or whelks, inserting their vulnerable soft bodies into the snaily convolutions. If you found one unsuspecting and relaxed, its claws would be resting outside the shell, disproportionately long and gnarled, and crossed like the hands of old ladies. But as soon as you touched it, in they would go, pulled back until all you could see were the pink horny tips crowded into the mouth of the shell. The surprising thing about these little creatures was that, in spite of the massive movement of the sea over them, if you went back to the same pool at the next low tide the same crabs would be there, waiting patiently with their claws out.

Where did I get that patience, to lie face down on a damp rock, staring into a pool, until its every pebble and weed was familiar enough to recognise at the next low tide? I watched the tiny transparent shrimps, their rudimentary insides showing as a spasm of black tube, fish an inch long that hovered above the weed and darted into hiding no matter how slowly and carefully I put a finger into the water to touch them. I learned that if I pushed a limpet suddenly sideways without warning, it would slip off the rock and show its flat round sucker underneath, but that the merest touch on the top of the shell would cause it to cling immovably. Brown crabs the size of my thumbnail scuttled across the pools, and always there were the fleshy petals of the bloodsucker anemones to tease until they closed.

There were other things to do there. We climbed worn paths up the cliff behind the clubhouse, onto the headland separating us and Tynemouth. This we called the Camel's Back, as it stretched two muddy humps towards the sea, with a narrow neck of rock between them. We would take turns to run along the first hump and jump across to the next, a drop of forty feet or so on each side of us. The field at the top of this cliff, the Boat Field, was used for storing the fishing boats upside down in the worst of the winter, when they would be scraped and repainted. Here and there was a rotting relic, an irreparable skeleton. We could hide under the boats, either to play hide and seek, or to tease someone who was currently out of favour. On sunny days, one or two of the fishermen would sit on crab pots, mending nets. The patient movement of the hands as they knotted and twisted the fine cords was fascinating and soothing. It was pleasant to sit nearby, in the sun and salty breeze, watching, and chatting a little about school, or the daft things trippers from Newcastle had done recently, or 'How's yer mam?'

One day, Kit and I found a boy sitting on the cliff path with a fishing hook stuck in his knee. Because I was in the Brownies, I knew that the only way to get it out was to push it further in until its curve caused it to emerge through the flesh. If you tried to pull it out, its barb would prevent this, and cause worse damage. Somehow the boy would not allow us to try Baden-Powell's method, so we helped him to his feet and walked with him the quarter mile to Dr. Yeoman's surgery, a lengthy journey, as he was bent double and holding his knee with both hands all the way.

I believed at the time that rescuing people from danger and injury was a normal part of life. Bringing myself up on a constant diet of fictional heroism performed by children, from the Famous Five to Swallows and Amazons, I genuinely felt that it was only lack of opportunity that prevented my performing likewise. When I was taught at Brownies how to put arms in slings and construct a stretcher from two jackets and a pair of walking sticks, I knew it was just a matter of time before this knowledge would be called upon. So, I took for granted that at the swimming club we children were taught, by one of the fathers, the Holger Nielsen method of resuscitation, in which a drowning victim is laid face down and you pump their arms and press their back to restart breathing. In the water we were shown how to swim backwards holding the drowning person from behind, arms firmly under their elbows to stop them struggling.

There was plentiful evidence that this knowledge may come in handy. Because day-trippers behaved with ignorance of the sea and a certain amount of stupidity, and club members were at hand, rescues took place with some regularity. Pam and Jeff's father, 'Uncle' Tony, had several times pulled spluttering and gasping teenagers to shore. One morning my mother went to the club for coffee, and found herself alone. It was chilly, and a slight mist had started to blow off the sea. As she sat looking out over the water, she realised she could see a pair of arms clinging to the seaward side of the pier, and a wet head visible between the low waves that engulfed it. She ran out along the pier, where a frantic boy's face gaped up at her. On this outer side of the pier, the stone wall dropped straight for about seven feet, then sloped outwards at a slight angle. The boy was just managing to hold himself against the slope, but slipping with every wave. At intervals along the wall were strong iron rings used as occasional moorings. My mother tried to shout to him to grab for one of these, but he was too panic-stricken to understand. So she ran back to where she could slide down into the water above the rocks, swam to him and managed to push him to where they could both grasp one of the rings. She was not a particularly strong swimmer, and could do no more than hold him there. Luckily, by this time one or two more club members having arrived for coffee, she and the boy were seen. Within minutes two younger women and the club's life belt were in the water, and the boy was saved. To her amazement, when he managed to pull his shaky body upright, he was seen to be a teenager over six feet tall, against her slight five feet and an inch.

Although I remember this event proudly because it was unusual for her, at the time I simply felt that this had been a normal opportunity to put lifesaving strategies into practice. I probably wondered why she had not turned the boy onto his back and pulled him by the elbows round into the calm waters of the bay, in the way we had been taught. Clinging to an iron ring seemed a rather incomplete rescue.

My first opportunity came when I was nine, and was equally inadequate. I was drifting about the bay in the canoe, when I heard my name being called frantically. On the end of the south pier was one of the younger club children, Tansy I think, jumping about and pointing into the water. Floating calmly and gently on his back was a small child. He looked quite comfortable except that the water was clearly lapping over his face. I got to him with two strong pulls of the paddles, and grabbed one of his arms. Although he was little I could not drag him aboard without danger of capsizing, so I held him by the neck of his shirt and wobbled the paddle until we reached the bottom of the stone steps leading up to the end of the pier. He was clearly alive and well and screaming loudly. I pushed him towards the bottom step, assuming he would realise his rescue was now complete. To my surprise, instead of grabbing the step and climbing up, the moment I let go of his shirt, he sank like a stone. Fortunately my reaction was quick; I leaned over and grabbed his hair just before he fell out of reach. This time I realised he needed more encouragement to get ashore, so I slipped into the water to heave and push him until he was firmly on the step, and held him by the throat until Tansy came down and grabbed him. He was tiny, about four years old, and had been left alone on the end of the pier with a crab-line. Even then I thought his parents had a funny idea of what was suitable for little children to do at the seaside. A minute or two later, his father strolled along the pier, by which time we had got him to the top of the steps, still screaming. The man gave us a strange angry look, and said to the child, 'Why are you so wet?' I was more preoccupied with the fact that now the rescue was over, I had to dive back into the water in my clothes, and swim after the canoe, which had started to drift out into forbidden waters beyond the pier.

I am sorry to say that I learned little from this experience. A year or two later, staying at a holiday camp in Wales which had a swimming pool, I was again called frantically to the rescue of a small child, this time by my brother. I executed a dramatic long flat dive, which brought me to the drowning toddler's side, grabbed his clothing, hauled him to the side and let him go, whereupon he slid to the bottom at my feet. Again, I pulled him up by the hair. This time, the rescue had been seen by his parents, who bought me a box of chocolates. It was small consolation for the fact that it was such wet weather that my mother had to try to dry my favourite sweater in the oven of our caravan, and burned it.

In spite of all the watery activities, for adults the club was principally a sociable organisation, and therefore as much a problem as a pleasure for my parents. As far as my father was concerned, it was to be visited rarely. Other husbands did as their children did, coming straight from work to the beach. The station for the local train that ran between the coast and Newcastle was a few minutes walk from the sea, so by six o'clock the men would be striding down the slope to the beach, taking off their ties and jackets. Their wives would have the urn boiling, the sandwiches and ham salads unpacked onto the verandah tables. Each family kept a supply of crockery in cupboards under the urn, and there was a bit of mostly good-natured rivalry about setting an attractive table. All of this was a dilemma for my mother, so she would make sure that Kit and I had plenty to eat at children's teatime, when we arrived from school at four o'clock. Then by about five thirty, knowing my father would soon be getting off the train, she would pack up and go home, often leaving us to play for a while, then to make our own way.

After tea, children and fathers would play on the beach, rounders and cricket, or if the tide was right everyone would swim. Tea was a light meal; you knew that you should not swim after dinner.

The club members swimming as a group must have been an amusing spectacle to outsiders. All the mothers were wearing their sensible swimsuits, and rubber caps with petals to look like flowers. Men's and boy's trunks came up to the waist, and there were still one or two older men who wore black one-piece suits with a singlet-style top. Several of the men also wore smooth black rubber caps. Children dressed similarly. My favourite swimsuit was yellow rather woolly fabric with white dots, and I had a pink rubber cap with a strap that held it securely under my chin. Up to thirty of us would walk into the sea, to adult waist height, and hold hands in a circle. Then, because the water was invariably cold, to encourage everyone in we would sing a verse of 'Ring a ring of roses' at the tops of our voices. When it came to 'All fall down,' the whole circle would fall into the water backwards. After that, some would swim a few strokes then go out to get warm and dry, having received the benefit of a dose of seawater. Others were more serious; the distance of one hundred yards between the ends of the piers was a useful stretch to measure your exercise. Across and back was considered a respectable distance. The children played until they were shivering. We had an inner tube from a lorry tyre, which we rolled down from the club into the sea. If you had it to yourself you could lie across it, supported at neck and knees, enjoying the movement of the water. But this reverie would invariably be broken by one of the other children jumping onto the side of the tube and tipping you out. So, you would wait a few moments and do the same in return.

There was one really dedicated swimmer. Everyone admired Mr. Clark; looking back I doubt his sanity. He did not socialise or have tea, although he was a pleasant friendly man. He swam. Every day, throughout the year, unless the weather was really against him, he would set off out to sea with a steady stroke, accompanied by his dog, a sturdy Labrador named Bruce. They would be gone a long time, the two sleek black heads disappearing towards the horizon. In summer, this seemed simply admirable if unnecessary; in winter, beyond comprehension. I could understand some of his explanation of why the water temperature changes very little through the year, but anyone seeing him breasting the inhospitable grey rollers under a steely sleety sky in February must have thought him mad.

Summer days were a different matter. Several of the women would meet at the club for coffee in the mornings, especially those who were the keener swimmers. I don't think anyone regularly stayed all day, but by mid-afternoon the deck chairs would be out. Sitting with your back to the pier wall, facing west, gave the best of the afternoon sun. Sheltered from any sea breeze, this spot was the most likely to be warm, and most of the club ladies were deeply tanned, their chests above the tops of their cotton sundresses the colour of conkers. The fact that my mother was always pale signified something of her uncertain status. Her deck chair was there, stored under the stairs in the clubhouse along with everyone else's. Indeed she was there, but she did not have the confidence to simply take her place, sit in it and join in the chatter, or the friendly silences. She was too afraid of being shown to be outside that magic circle. So she would sit for a while, go in and fuss around the urn, get tea ready for us, sit with us while we ate it, fuss around some more, then find it was time to go. On days when only one or two others were there, she was more comfortable, and somehow made a point of being friendly towards the less regular attendees. Yet these women were her friends, they invited her to their houses, they were funny and hospitable, and alone with each individual she was fine. I know this because she so often took me with her. I don't recall that she openly boasted about my success at school, but she assumed it was known. Pam, daughter of one of those magical Smith sisters, was in my class, so surely it was reported that I had come first in the weekly tests again. Probably no one was especially aware or more than briefly interested, but to my mother I was the talisman, the entry into the sphere of admired ones. So my presence as a reminder was useful. I did not mind; I liked listening to women's conversation.

As well as having my school reputation to maintain, I soon acquired another, as a swimmer. From four years old onwards, I swam confidently and strongly, and the club offered the opportunity for me to demonstrate my expertise, in the form of the annual Gala. This was held each September, in part marking the end of the season in which all the regulars would go to the beach every day, rain or shine. For the Gala, on a Sunday afternoon, we borrowed the premises of Tynemouth Swimming Club. This was a very different swimming environment, for it was an almost indoor, freshwater pool in North Shields, on Hawkeys Lane. The pool itself was open to the sky, and unheated, but around it were covered seating areas. It felt very uncomfortable to us, as it was chlorinated, which we found much stingier to the eyes than seawater. Also, being fresh water, it was less buoyant, and felt like much harder work to swim in. The handicaps affected all equally, however, and it was possible to have races that we could not have staged in the waters of the bay.

The events were taken seriously; breaststroke, free-style (crawl as we referred to it), and backstroke races for girls, for boys, for women, for men, over various distances. Then there were relays for each group; finally, some more light-hearted events, such as obstacle or dressing up races. Some people did not take part at all. Only the younger mothers, for instance, joined in; 'women' really meant older girls, above the age of thirteen or fourteen. Most of the older generation of men kept their clothes on as spectators, especially the ones with titles such as President and Chairman of the club.

I started taking part in the girls' races when I was seven. At that time, there was an older girl, I remember only as Olga, who swam sleek and fast, and was reputed to be accustomed to the strange flat water of the pool. I do not remember her being at the beach ever, but she must have been a member of the club, for she turned up for the Gala year after year. My first year, I came second to her in all the events, which felt fine, and was enough to please my mother, for Olga was known to be a phenomenal swimmer. The second year, to my surprise, I beat her easily.

My mother was quietly ecstatic. She did not praise me, in case I became vain, but accepted praise of me in a quiet, self-effacing way. It was almost as if she had won the events herself and was trying to appear modest. I was scared. I realised in a confused, partly conscious way, that I had another set of difficult targets to live up to now. Not only was I to be well behaved, self-controlled and top of the class, I had also to be the best swimmer.

Olga made it easy for me for two or three years, by moving up into the women's events. Amongst the girls that were left to compete with me, I wish I had not to try so hard. I wish it could have continued to be fun so that we could have shared the successes, but swimming had become serious business for me, as part of my mother's armour against rejection. By the time I followed Olga into the women's races when I was eleven or twelve (there was no point my competing with eight-year-olds in the girls' races) I was swimming for the county, and the responsibility imposed by my mother's needs made it a miserable chore. I still remember those first sparkling moments with the bright foaming waves around me on a summer day, the joy and freedom of flying in the buoyant water, and it does not seem like the same activity at all.

Friends & Other Children

My first friend was Maureen, who lived a few houses away along our street. The semi-detached pair, of which hers was one, was unusual in being newer than all the other houses. This was because that place had been hit by a bomb, the original houses destroyed, and the space filled up again after the war. In layout these houses were the same, but in appearance subtly different. The woodwork was less sturdy, the colour of the bricks lighter and less uniform. So, if not a scar, a reminder stood in the street of what had gone before. Not that it was mentioned much in our house, of course. The silence on the subject meant that I took for granted in my childhood that ordinary suburban streets could receive that kind of onslaught, and that somehow it did not matter.

Once, I went home and told my mother that I had seen an old man with a beard sitting on a chair outside Maureen's front door. For a little while she believed, with a mixture of excitement and horror, that I had seen the ghost of the man who had been killed by the bomb. Then she found out that Maureen's grandfather had come to stay for a few weeks, and he was in the habit of sitting at his doorstep, chatting with passers-by. This put my mother in a quandary. She liked Maureen, who was a gentle, sweet-natured child. She liked Maureen's mother; although she wore her hair a little too long and loose, she was a quiet and shy person. Maureen's parents spoke with an accent, but it was not a Geordie accent; they came from Liverpool. So the usual guidelines for assessing social acceptability were difficult to apply. However, an elderly member of the family putting a chair at the front door, and sitting there with a rug over his lap, had rather a strong flavour of the Irish peasant stock which was undoubtedly in their background. For myself, I thought it was a bit embarrassing that he was so ready to engage strangers in conversation, but I was aware of my mother's irritation by the number of times she muttered about how much more suitable it would be for him to sit in the back garden. 'What do they think back gardens are for?' she asked herself plaintively whenever she had been drawn into a comment about the weather on her way home from the shops.

Eventually the old man was collected by Maureen's aunt and taken back home to Liverpool, and my friendship settled back into its unthreatening normality. Our back garden was more interesting than Maureen's, having steps to run up and down, or to sit on. We had a bit more lawn, my bit of flower bed to grub around in, and a place in one corner where it was possible to hide in the lower growth of a lilac tree that had pushed its way through from the garden beyond the end of ours. So my memory is of us always playing in my garden rather than hers. In those first memories of playing there, I was probably four. I have a photograph of Maureen, and myself at that age, sitting on the steps with what appear to be mud pies in front of us. But she was two years older than I, which meant that our friendship had a shaky foundation, as I could not always offer the same fun as being with other older children. At the end of the street, in the last house on the corner, lived another Maureen, the same age, and sometimes the two would exclude me from their activities. I can remember how I felt about this. I was horribly jealous, and carried a burning weight of tears and anger in my chest when I saw my Maureen pass our gate on her way to the other. But I felt there must be some magic link between them because of the coincidence of their name and age. It was as if they were twins. Also, I became convinced that there was an inferiority in me that would prevent me from properly joining in their games. This was because in the front garden of Maureen no.2 was a huge mature sycamore tree, with massive spreading black branches. Both Maureens could climb into the tree and sit high above my head, while I looked up at the swinging soles of their sandals. I knew that I could not do this, was scared to try, and this proved that they had an affinity that I could never share.

There was another rift between us, in that they went together into

Whitley Bay to the Saturday morning cinema, a show put on especially for children. The cinema was referred to as 'going to the pictures'. I believe other people of my generation have fond memories of Flash Gordon and Roy Rogers, but I was not allowed to go. Maybe my mother decided the sixpence it cost was better spent elsewhere, but the tone in which the shows were mentioned indicated quite clearly that Saturday morning cinema was 'common'. She was skilful in her expressing of these opinions. Never could I have reported to anyone that they, or their appearance, or their behaviour were unacceptable, because the judgement was never explained. It was a sniff, a flicker of the eyebrows. Sometimes it was a single word; 'Oh, *her...*' would be enough to show the person to be beneath our notice. And I trusted the judgement, therefore shared it. Sometimes it irritated me. Once, for instance, a very jolly new girl joined our class at Infants School. She was confident, lively, funny, and everyone's friend. I really wanted to join in, but it was clear she was not for me. She smelled of wet pants and unwashed hair, but this was quite overcome by the force of her personality. At the time, I was convinced that the way in which she betrayed her inferiority was that her cardigan tied at the neck with a cord sporting large coloured pompons on the ends. Another child was seen off similarly. She and her family lived on our street for a while, but she never made it into the circle of friends because the ribbon bows in her hair were too large.

As a result of my indoctrination, I never really wanted to go to the pictures, except that I felt left out. The two Maureens were not the only ones to go from our street. I believed that I understood the experience of the cinema. Sometimes when I went shopping in Newcastle with my Grandma, she would take me to a little cinema called the News Theatre. I think it had that name because during the war it had shown the Pathe Newsreel several times a day. By the time I was being taken there in the late 40s and early 50s the programme was continuous cartoons, Mickey Mouse, Donald Duck and Tweety Pie usually, in my memory. I enjoyed it, as an occasional treat, but could understand that there was no reason to go every week.

Suddenly, and frighteningly as it happened, the rule was relaxed. In our street lived Sheila and Claire, known as the 'big girls'. When I was about five, they were ten or eleven. One afternoon, the two of them offered to take a number of the younger children, including me, to see, not the children's programme, but a real film. This was 'Against All Flags', starring Errol Flynn and Maureen O'Hara. It was a story of pirates, filmed in what was, to me, startlingly vivid colour, and grotesquely close-up detail. Until then, of course, in that time before television, all the entertainment I had seen on screen was in the form of what were clearly nothing more than moving drawings. I had never seen real people involved in the stories, and did not understand about acting. My visits to the pantomime had not prepared me for it, as the characters on stage, amid painted scenery, were surrounded by obvious pretence, unlike what appeared now. I watched aghast as men in strange clothes punched and knifed each other, swung terrifyingly in the rigging of ships tossed on gigantic waves, and attempted to cut off each other's heads with flashing, swishing swords. The immediacy of the action kept me rigid and open-mouthed, but suspense I could not bear. A scene came in which the hero and heroine (Flynn and O'Hara) had been captured by the pirates and were refusing to give some information, probably the vital clue for the finding of the treasure. In order to persuade them to talk, the two of them were dragged, struggling, to a beach, where they were bound hand and foot to a pair of massive stakes at the shoreline. So far, frightening enough, then to my utter horror, from the sea came crabs, a hundred times the size of crabs I knew, crabs bigger than Maureen O'Hara's foot, which they began to bite with their claws.

'You'll stay there until you are nothing but bones,' promised the pirate captain, whereupon I slipped from my seat to crouch on the floor. The big girls realised I was scared, and one of them held my head down until the scene was over, an unnecessary precaution, as I had no intention of coming up again. I suppose they escaped the crabs and the pirates, but I did not care to find out.

These older children eased my way into exploring beyond our street. In a way, I led two lives. At the beach, my mother was usually present, and the freedom of the shore and the water was quickly achieved, but mostly under her eye, or that of other swimming club parents. Playing in the street, and eventually beyond, happened with her in the house, busy, leaving me to the devices of my friends. Across the street, round the corner, Broadway, the road from Whitley Bay to Tynemouth was the boundary between town and country. On our side, the four tidy streets, the railway line, the old village, the sea. On the other side, fields. There was a stone walled farmhouse set back from the road, but we never thought that the fields belonged to anyone. Not far from the first fence that we climbed was a shallow pond, in spring filled with masses of frog spawn twitching and glinting in the sunlight. It was our destructive way of studying nature to take jar after jar of the spawn home, or to school, to watch it die and fester into a stinking green sludge. Similarly we scoured the hedges for nests and eggs, believing that a blue or speckled egg, kept warm in a pocket for an hour or two, would hatch into a pet bird to keep.

The nearest we ever came to success was in the case of the green and yellow caterpillars gathered from under the leaves of the hedges, which, if kept in a jar with some of the same leaves, would sometimes turn into glossy brown chrysalids, but never make the next phase into butterflies.

There were boys in our group, too. Sheila's brother Ian, and Claire's brother, John, a couple of years older than I was, took cricket bat and ball, or waded in the pond in their wellingtons. I was happy to make daisy chains, or watch small insects in the grass. By this time, I had another friend from round the corner on Longston Avenue, Sandra, (not the one who squashed the rat), my own age and in my class at school. With her I ventured further. Beyond the field with the pond, a deep cut green lane bordered a cornfield. Here we made a den in the hedgerow by wriggling under the prickly hawthorn into a dry ditch, which we lined with grass and straw from the field. One day, making our way to the den, we saw someone was there already. Sandra grabbed my arm, and, crouching down, pulled me over the lane, into the tall barley. 'It's her next door,' she mouthed almost silently into my ear. From our vantage point on the high side of the lane, we could see Sandra's teenaged neighbour lying in our den with her boyfriend. My view was rather blocked by Sandra's obviously indignant back, but I could see a disarrangement of clothes, and certain movements of the bodies.

'What are they doing?' I asked, something above a whisper. Immediately, the boyfriend's head shot up, and before we could so much as move, he was towering over us, holding a stick. His face, especially around his mouth, was very red. I wondered if he knew. Although I felt that his appearance made him look silly rather than cross, I was scared.

'Get out of here, you filthy bitches,' he snarled, and swiped at us with his stick. Still keeping her head low, out of sight of the neighbour, Sandra pulled us away. Once we had scuttled a good distance, she slowed down.

'That's no way to talk to girls,' she said darkly. I had a feeling she knew something I didn't, but then her father was a policeman, which I realised gave an insight into all kinds of naughtiness that had nothing to do with us.

Not far away in this stretch of countryside was a disused quarry. I don't know what had been dug from there, or how long since it had been used. The Victorian pub that stood nearby was called the Quarry Inn, so it must have been of some age. Its banks were overgrown, its steep sides covered in a tangled mass of bramble and elder, and there was water at the bottom. Along one side of its perimeter, where it bordered the Broadway, there was a stone wall, about eight or ten feet high. Another side was inaccessible where the buildings and yards of the farm ran alongside it. But, when approached from the fields, or indeed along part of a residential street that overlooked one edge, it was easy to gain access. There was nothing more than a four-strand barbed wire fence, and the thorny brambles. Of course, going anywhere near such a dangerous place was totally forbidden. In fact, it was so forbidden that it was never mentioned to me, so self-evidently dangerous that no one, even a child, would dream of attempting to cross the walls or fences.

Naturally, it was an interesting place to visit. I don't remember climbing through the fence just for the sake of defiance, and never went alone. At the back end of the summer, all children went blackberrying; it was part of the natural cycle of living within reach of the countryside. For us the best blackberries grew in the tangle surrounding the quarry. So the big girls would lead us in, holding the barbs of the fence up over our heads to keep us safe. Then we were marshalled into a group, told to keep close, and set about filling paper bags, our pockets, or, I remember in my case, the tin bucket I used to take to the beach. When we could carry no more, we climbed out again, and took the spoils home. I was not asked where I had been. My mother, I suppose, thought we had gleaned the hedgerows along the green lane or around the field with the pond, almost close enough to be within calling distance. In any case, she trusted the big girls, who were so sensible.

When I was six or seven, I was given a set of large books, wonderful books, called The World of the Children. There were four big volumes, covering a host of interesting and educational topics, mostly presented in the form of stories. Some covered mathematical or scientific topics; for instance, in one of these tales, some children had an interesting uncle who showed them how to calculate the depth of a well by dropping a stone down it and timing the interval until the sound of the splash. Another, in a set about literature, had a story of a man who made a library for children out of an old railway carriage, and described the books that were favourites. There were pages of instructions for folding paper into hats and boxes and birds, and Chinese junks.

The four volumes of The World of the Children covered Art and manners, good and bad strangers, science and sums, all as stories. I adored them, and devoured them, but my favourite section was about nature and the countryside. The stories here were of a town girl, Jennifer, going to live in the country, making friends with a gamekeeper's son called Robert, who told her the names of birds and flowers, animals and trees. I felt there was an element of romance in their relationship, and I was fascinated by the variety of things it was possible to see and learn in the fields and woods.

I had no gamekeeper's son to accompany me, but I had Sandra, and sometimes Maureen, though she was less adventurous, less inclined to stray from home, in spite of her greater age. Sandra and I found that the undisturbed area around the quarry was a rich source of the plants and creatures we wanted to find. We had I-spy books of Birds, Trees and Flowers, and ticked off the species with enthusiasm and little accuracy. Cautious of the watery depths of the quarry, we crept around its highest edges, looking for hearts-ease, scarlet pimpernels, coltsfoot and celandines. Back at home on wet days, we made scrap books containing squashed examples of these flowers, pressed between sheets of toilet paper, and carefully named, which crumbled to dust over the winter, and had to be replaced. It was beautiful on warm days, the occasional sound of a car on the Broadway muffled by the canopy of trees, blending with insect drones and the wash of breeze in the branches. Occasionally, boys would come in gangs, to jump shouting down the banks, swearing at the ripping of the brambles, to throw stones down into the water.

We had places to hide, peeping out from the undergrowth until they moved on. Sometimes we knew them, boys not much older than we were, recognised from school, but in their groups of eight or ten they seemed so much stronger and louder, so much more in command of their surroundings. We walked delicately in that place, careful of the possibility of falling into the dark water, which held a threat I never felt in the waters of the sea. To those of us well acquainted with it, the sea was open with its danger. Depth came gradually; you could walk towards it and judge it. Storms announced them-selves with noise and violent movement; you could stay away. But the water of the quarry was black and reflective and still, its depth hidden. The sides were steep, almost vertical at the edge, so that if you fell it could be impossible to find a foothold to climb out. You would scrabble and slip until your strength ran out. But the boys ran and jumped on the steeply sloping banks. They shouted their way through the undergrowth, and scrambled down to the water's edge on tenuous paths made partly of stones embedded in the wall and partly of the matted tangle of brambles.

One day a group of them found us. We had hidden in a depression under one of the best blackberry bushes, the thorny branches curving above us. But one of us was wearing a bright yellow cardigan, and the colour caught the eye of a tall red-haired boy as he stamped his way through the bushes nearby. Pausing, he looked at us without moving or speaking for several seconds, and we peered back in silence, hoping he would leave us and go. But with a shout he summoned the rest of the gang and we were pulled out, scratched and scared.

The boys jostled round us. One of them lost his balance and slid on the slope, pushing Sandra off her feet. Together they slipped almost to the water's edge.

'Watchit! You'll fall in,' another one shouted.

'Push 'er in anyway.' The fallen boy climbed back up, leaving Sandra crouched below. At this point the bank was less steep; she was able to keep her footing, but seemed frightened to move back up towards us.

'Throw 'em both in,' another one shouted.

'We can swim,' I said, with more bravado than I felt. Actually I did not know whether Sandra could swim. She was not one of the Swimming Club children, and rarely went to the beach.

Answering back centred the attention on me. One of them pushed me backwards into the brambles. As I scrambled to my feet again, I felt the tearing of the thorns on the backs of my thighs.

'Stop it,' I shouted. 'That hurts. I'm bleeding.'

One of the boys, whose face I knew, but not his name, tried to break away from the rest of the gang.

'Come away,' he said, quietly. 'Leave them alone.' For a moment they wavered, one or two of them starting to climb up the bank away from us. The red-haired boy stopped them.

'Not till we've seen them swim,' he said, grinning. Sandra had scuffled sideways along the bank. She was still crouching, silent and terrified, but out of reach. The tall boy pulled me down to the water's edge, balancing with one foot braced in a tangle of branches. I was too frightened of falling to struggle, and merely tried to hold myself rigid in his grasp, leaning back into the bank. With a swift dextrous movement he grabbed me by one arm and leg, and tipped me over so he was holding me above the water by my ankles. Ridiculously, I tried to hold my skirt so that it did not fall over my head, exposing my knickers. For a moment or two, I could hear shouting and laughter from close by, then there was a sudden silence as my head and shoulders were plunged into the water. The shock of the cold made me twist and kick, breaking one foot free of his grasp, so that for another second or two I dangled helplessly. I think my arms were attempting a swimming motion, and I was terribly aware of a rushing, pulsing noise in my ears, as I struggled to twist my body up, and my head out of the water. The moment when he dropped me, and I slid down into a greenish darkness, then kicked straight up into the sunlight, was an ecstatic relief. I kicked twice, feeling the cling of my skirt, and the unexpected weight of my sandals, and grasped a branch. Above my head, sounds of crashing and shouting indicated the flight of the gang, except the red-haired boy. He leaned down, grabbed my wrist, and heaved me back up to where I could pull on the grass and brambles to get myself out of the water.

'Stupid kid! Yer shoulda kept still. I wasn't going to drop you,' he yelled into my face. He turned to Sandra, who was already reaching across to help me. 'Grab 'er arm,' he shouted. I was safely on the bank by now, but I gripped her hand tightly anyway.

Just then, a wordless shout from above startled him by its urgency. He turned, leaping and scrambling up and out of sight.

'What's going on? Who's down there?' a man's voice called. Sandra and I crouched in silence, terrified of being caught in the quarry grounds. The voice shouted again, but by now the boys had all escaped and silence fell. Birdsong broke into my consciousness; I shivered and felt the sting of the scratches that covered most of my body. After a few minutes, when the uninterrupted sounds of wind in the trees, birds, and a car droning by on the road above convinced us that we were alone again, we slowly crept up to the roadside, under the wire, and made for home.

Sandra was relatively unscathed, but shocked and crying. Her legs were scratched, but not much more than usual. My case was different. Wet from head to foot so that my clothes clung to me, I shivered so that my teeth clattered against each other and I could barely walk. Down the backs of my legs, streams of blood ran from long deep scratches, barely diluted by the water, so that the tops of my socks became soaked with red. Where I had been pulled through the brambles, not just my skin, but the back of my skirt had been ripped, so that a wide triangle of the fabric flapped and clung across the backs of my bleeding legs.

'What are we going to say?' I asked, still convinced that the worst of our trouble lay in it being found out that we had gone into the quarry.

'We'll have to tell,' she wept.

'No,' I replied. 'We'll get into trouble. I can say I fell in the pond.'

'But you're all ripped,' she pointed out.

'I'll say some boys chased us and I fell in the hedge, then in the pond.'

It was the best I could think of. My mother was shocked by my appearance, as I limped into the kitchen. Having cleaned me up, anointed my scratches with Zambuk, and put dry clothes on me, she took me round to speak to Sandra's mother in an attempt to find out who the chasing boys could be. Since we could only say with honesty that we did not know them, the story was accepted. Unfortunately, as we could not be so honest about where it had happened, we were both forbidden to play in the pond field or the green lane, so for the time being our nature study came to an end.

A couple of years later, when Sandra and I were ten or eleven, two boys were less fortunate. By then, we were keen tennis players, and spent many an afternoon on a court in Tynemouth Park, lobbing slow balls across the net. One day, Douglas and Chris, from our class at school, appeared at the side of the court, and peered at us through the mesh wall. Failing to engage us in conversation, as we were more interested in our game than their ten-year-old badinage, Douglas decided to shoot us with an air pistol he was carrying. He wasn't a bad shot, and in the space of a few seconds had hit both of us two or three times on our bare legs. The impacts stung like wasp stings, and instantly came up like bright red peas on our skin. One on Sandra's thigh drew blood. Then the two of them ran off.

We went home to Sandra's house, stung both in body and temper. We expected sympathy and indignation, but I for one was surprised by the speed with which the incident escalated. Because we were so used to the idea that we took it for granted, we had not thought of the fact that Sandra's father was a police sergeant. He had just come home, and was sitting drinking tea, his boots off and his uniform jacket unbuttoned, but as soon as he saw our injuries, his boots and helmet were on, and he was out of the house on his way back to the station. In this case we could name names, and had done so before the implication of his position had even dawned on us.

A few weeks later, Sandra and I found ourselves giving evidence in the juvenile court, an experience that I found terrifying, although we were treated gently and kindly. We were told that we must address our answers to the magistrate, who sat in silence at a high bench, even though the questions were posed by a lady who stood near us in the court. I found it terribly difficult to turn away from the questioner, and could speak only with a quivering voice. I was convinced that my ineptitude was getting me into trouble. Also, by then I had passed an exam which would enable me to go to a very selective and desirable girls' school in Newcastle, and my mother had sent me to the court in my brand new and over-large uniform. She wanted me to impress, but I felt so strange and uncomfortable, not myself at all.

Anyway, back when our first adventure restricted us to the streets outside our homes, Sandra and I learned to roller-skate. Our skates were metal ones, metal wheels on metal plates that strapped to the bottoms of our shoes. We skated and skated, until we acquired red calluses across the fronts of our ankles where the straps chafed, and until the metal of the wheels wore through and silver ball bearings ran out. Also, we became skilful, able to glide along on one foot, the other raised behind like a ballet dancer, able to turn and jump and twirl. Of course, there was little traffic on the streets, and the few drivers who used them were accustomed to the fact that the roads were playgrounds for children.

Meanwhile, I was still playing with Maureen and others of the older children. I enjoyed their company, although some of the games had little meaning for me. One was a variation on grandmother's footsteps, which required the knowledge of the names of famous film stars. One person would stand on one pavement, the rest on the opposite side of the road. The one would shout out initials, and the first person to shout out the name could take one step forward. I had no idea who Gloria Swanson, Rita Hayworth, John Wayne or Robert Taylor were, but in due course I learned the names and could join in.

Another game saw a row of four or five children standing on top of the garden wall, throwing balls at an empty can containing twenty or so lolly sticks. As soon as the can was hit, everyone jumped down to gather the sticks. The winner was the one who picked up most sticks. I remember this game because on one occasion, when the can went over, and I made my dive for it, my feet slipped backwards over the wall, I fell forwards, and dragged my shins painfully down the front edge of the bricks. There was copious bleeding, so that by the time I had run the thirty or so yards to my own front gate, my feet were slipping about on the blood inside my shoes.

These street games taught me how friendship could be fickle and shifting. Sandra was always my friend, but sometimes she was Jean's also, sometimes Jean's best friend was Alma. Pam, from the Swimming Club, came from her home on the other side of the Broadway to visit her grand-mother in Houghton Avenue, and when this happened she was Jean's best friend. But at the club she was mine. Occasionally, they would all be occupied with each other; I would feel left out and hate them. Next day we would all be hand in hand, swooping in circles on our skates.

We played games that have probably disappeared into history. Hopscotch, because our pavements were laid with stone slabs in an alternating bond that matched the pattern of a hopscotch court. Chucks, or jacks, with little cubes of coloured chalky stone, or made of metal with six little legs, that required the skill and dexterity to throw one high, and pick up one, or two or three, before catching the first one. Two-ball, throwing the balls against a wall, with variations, bouncing one under your knee, or round your back. We skipped, either alone or as a group. Skipping alone involved being able to skip a simple jump, bounce, long, short, rhythm, or turning the rope fast to jump every time it came round. Or skipping with the rope turning backwards, or with crossed arms. Skipping in groups needed a turner at each end of the rope, and there were endless variations. My favourite could be done with a minimum of six skippers, each of whom skipped across the rope once in turn, the whole line making a figure of eight around the two who were turning. Even the lamp posts provided a game that has now gone. They were old gas lamps, converted for electricity, but still with the two sturdy arms at the top, designed for the lamplighter's ladder. We slung our rope on these arms, and swung in a spiral around the post. Remembering this puts me in mind of the nursery rhyme 'Boys and girls come out to play, The moon doth shine as bright as day…', because we did play out after dark, swinging around the lamp post. Probably it was just five o'clock on a winter's afternoon, but the darkness gave it a glamour that sticks in the memory.

More
School

My experience in Class 4A, the year 1956 to 1957, was probably the culmination of the confusion, anguish and pleasure that had been building during my years at Cullercoats School. From age five, or even before, I had been aware of that need to excel, the responsibility placed on me for my mother's peace of mind. Already, when I was just six, the secrecy with which I had guarded my sacking from the job of milk monitor shows that I had learned the necessity for deceit. In my mind, almost in the vibration of my nerves, I carried this double, overlapping image of my own self. Clearly, almost simplistically, drawn was the perfect, and therefore loveable, daughter of my mother's need. She was a pleasant-looking child, pale of complexion but sturdy and healthy, straight-limbed and tall enough. Her hair, regretfully acknowledged as straight in a Shirley Temple world where lovely children had golden curls, was nevertheless sleek, dark and shiny. She was neat and well-dressed. Above all, she was a composite of accomplishments, top of the class, captain of the team, artist, dancer, musician. Behind her, visible as it were a shadowy reflection, stood the secret reality, the less appealing child I knew myself to be. Even to myself, the two were sometimes hard to distinguish. The shadowy imperfect girl did have many of the skills and achievements displayed by the clear perfect one; much of the time she could slide the shadow almost into the bright image, rather like a ghostly soul rejoining its body. But always there was that secret discrepancy that hung as a weight, the knowledge that it could only be maintained through deceit, through the pretence that it was possible to be that perfect one.

Our daily and weekly routines in 4A underpinned the image of accomplishment. Every evening we were given ten spellings to learn, and these were tested the next morning. I was fortunate in having an excellent visual memory; I never needed to learn spellings because the appearance of a word would fix in my mind's eye. So my daily spelling test score was unfailingly ten out of ten. Then we did the regular mental arithmetic test. Although it was plain that my natural strengths involved words, and I found it more difficult to work reliably with numbers, there were skills and tricks I had learned which helped me. The sound and rhythm of chanting tables had fixed those patterns in my head. Here also my visual ability helped. I could see in my mind's eye a stream of numbers regimented by tens, so adding and subtracting was a matter of dancing backwards and forwards through the lines. Our teacher, Mr. Fisher, would call out the sum, and you quickly wrote down your answer (no working out on paper allowed) in your Mental Arithmetic book. Sometimes I got one wrong, but then most people found this the most challenging test, and I managed to keep ahead.

As my passion was reading, it could be supposed that this would be my favourite classroom activity. In fact I found it boring. Every day, at least half an hour would be spent reading aloud in turn. The class was large, and the range of skill somewhat diverse, so a considerable time would be spent listening to other children gabbling or stumbling through the story. One's own turn was short, if Mr. Fisher was in a patient mood, therefore willing to give the poorer performers more practice, or longer if he found the stumbling harder to tolerate. I managed my boredom by rapidly reading ahead, with a finger in the page involving the rest of the class. This was fine until I reached the end of the book about a fortnight ahead and had it all to read again several times over. Shades of Noddy in Toytown.

With my considerable experience of how the inside of a storybook should sound, I had no difficulty with Composition. In an hour spent writing, style heavily plagiarised from Lorna Hill or Elinor Brent Dyer, tales of ballerinas and boarding schools, hunting and ponies, would flow from my pen. Why these unoriginal offerings appealed to Mr. Fisher I do not know; he gave me full marks, ten out of ten, week after week. Maybe he never read girls' books and didn't recognise the stories, maybe he was impressed by my perfect spelling and convoluted sentence structure. Part of the pleasure of the Composition book lay in trying to write as much as possible while maintaining the most beautiful style of handwriting. The flowing loopy curves we had been taught, little changed since Victorian copybooks, I found satisfying to perform and lovely to look at. Our pens had long steel nibs clipped onto straight wooden handles, and we dipped them into the white china inkwells nestled in the corners of our desks. Some people stuffed their inkwells with pieces of torn blotting paper in order to have horribly messy missiles to flick around the room. This was pointless. The activity was theoretical, an idea gleaned from Billy Bunter books. It may have been possible amongst the boys of Greyfriars, but not in the ordered rows of Class 4A Cullercoats Junior School.

Every week on Friday morning, more serious tests were carried out. A selection of the week's spellings was followed by a written Arithmetic test, problems this time. These were of the nature of 'A train travelling at sixty-two miles per hour takes four and three-quarter hours to travel from Newcastle to London. What is the distance?' This time the sum had to be presented as exercises in multiplication and division, with every step shown. In an attempt, I suppose, to make the exercises seem relevant to life, the next one could carry on the story. ' The full fare is fifteen shillings. How much would it cost for a family of two adults and three children to make the journey?' Also there would be a page of long division and long multiplication sums. I was a little more worried by these, because it was possible that one small slip would destroy the perfect result that I needed. Sums based in money or measurement were the trickiest. We were working with two hundred and forty pennies or twenty shillings in a pound, multiples of half crowns and florins, even guineas. On the backs of our exercise books were tables of fathoms and furlongs, tables showing the number of inches in a cubit, the relationship of rods to poles and perches, and the fact that a chain (66 feet or 22 yards) was the length of the wicket in cricket. So, chanting the song that said 'Twelve inches in a foot, three feet in a yard, one thousand seven hundred and sixty yards in a mile' seemed easy by comparison. I regret the loss of the words, but not the complexities of the numbers.

To the results of the maths and spelling tests were added the week's mark for Composition, a handwriting exercise (which I enjoyed because of the curvy copperplate), and for recitation. Strangely, because I loved reading, and had several books of poetry given to me by my grandma, recitation bothered me most. Something had changed in me since the days when I memorised Jim and the Lion, or the simple arithmetical rules of the infants' school. Now, I found it more difficult to learn words accurately by heart. Remembering quite complex information (one hearing of a radio programme on the life cycle of the honeybee for instance) posed no problem. Working methods, say in arithmetic, I could apply reliably once I had understood. The content, rhythm and significant phrases of a poem would stick in my mind easily. But rote learning of a whole chunk of its text threatened to elude me. We were expected to choose a poem of at least twenty lines and recite it from memory to the class. I never lost marks for speaking with expression, but by choosing always something of the minimum required length I irritated Mr. Fisher and he would often refuse to give me more than 9 out of 10 no matter how perfect my delivery.

These tests, plus marks for Reading and Composition, were collated into a week's score, with the outcome that I was almost always first or second in the class. My rivals were Alec and Christine, but it was friendly rivalry, on my part anyway. I knew that if one of them beat me, the chances were that I would overcome again next week. The important results were the termly exams and reports, because it was those that were made known at home. I had to be first then.

The competition between Christine, Alec and myself needed to be friendly, because the most obvious outcome of the tests was that we sat in the classroom in the order of our results. The room was a Victorian galleried class; in other words the floor was stepped up from the front like a lecture theatre, with the desks in rows on the steps. My customary first place was top left, as seen from the front, so I would invariably be sitting next to Alec or Christine. I cannot imagine how it must have felt always to be sitting in the seats at the bottom right, bottom of the class for all the world to see. It was bad enough for me when one week, after I had been away with a cold for a couple of days (my mother still tended to mollycoddle my nasal passages), I came third. I was sitting in that shameful position, when in came Mr. Freeman, the headmaster. He glanced across at me and feigned exaggerated shock and horror at seeing me there. I was too much overcome by my genuine sense of humiliation and despair to realise that he was joking. There was a Class 4B also, set out in the same way, with some poor child sitting bottom right in that classroom too.

In our class, 4A, there were fifty-one pupils sitting in those rows, all, as far as I remember, kept in perfect silent order by Mr. Fisher. He had three strategies in maintaining this regime. The first was that we were kept busy. Every moment of every day was filled with a clearly defined and strictly timed activity; half an hour for sums, an hour for composition, an hour for art, half an hour in the yard for drill, forty minutes listening to a radio programme, twenty minutes answering questions about it, in writing of course. So it went on. The second strategy was that the rule of silence did not waver. It was easy to remember to be quiet, because it was always a requirement, except during the chanting of tables or other rules to be memorised. Working together, in pairs or groups, as is customary in schools nowadays, was unthinkable to Mr. Fisher.

The third strategy at his disposal was the cane. This was not a theoretical threat, it was a daily part of our lives. The implement itself, a yellow tapering stick a yard long, lay along the shelf at the bottom of the blackboard. Some of the time, he would hold it in his hand, using it as a pointer when working on the board, and giving it an occasional cracking swish, just to remind us. There was an extensive list of misdeeds that would result in the application of the cane to your person, hands or bottom for boys, hands only for girls. Being late was the first and most likely misdemeanour. One boy, David, was caned almost every day for this, a quick whack across each hand. He always cried a little, but then would be late again the next day. Mr. Fisher seemed not to notice that the punishment was ineffective. I believe that after a while he used David's lateness as an example, an excuse to demonstrate his willingness to control us all by the application of the cane. Teachers were allowed their moments of sadism in those days.

That we were afraid of it, there is no doubt. The small whackings that took place in the classroom were reputedly as nothing compared to those that were given by the Head. I do not remember any member of my class being caned by Mr. Freeman, but from time to time someone from the B stream was subjected to the more serious beating. Afterwards the child would have to go home. Perhaps this was in the way of temporary exclusion from school as part of the punishment, but we believed it was because the injuries were so severe.

One terrible day it was my turn. I had attempted to learn for recitation the story of the Minstrel Boy by Thomas Moore. It should have been easy, as I knew it as a song, and felt that I could keep the tune and the rhythm going in my head to carry me through. However, I had left the book at home by mistake, and this made me nervous. Other children took their turn at the front of the class, declaiming or mumbling or rattling their way through with various levels of success. I desperately muttered my words to myself over and over as I waited, anxiety prickling in my stomach. If I could get through without stumbling all would be well, but if I needed a prompt it would not be there. Too soon it was my turn. I started briskly;

'The minstrel boy to the war has gone,
In the..'
'Is,' said Mr. Fisher.
Startled, I began again, trying to comply with his interjection although it made no sense to me.
'The minstrel boy to the war has gone,
Is the ranks of death..'
More irritated now, he interrupted, 'No, no. Not *is* the ranks of death, *in* the ranks of death. Try to make it make sense.'
'Sorry. The minstrel boy to the war has gone,
In the ranks..'
'*Is*! *Is*! Not *has*! Listen to me.'

In my confusion I could not relate his instruction to anything I had said. Terrified of repeating my mistake I stood dumbly at the front of the classroom, unable to continue.
'Have you learned this poem at all, Elaine?' Mr. Fisher asked, exasperated. I suppose he was already annoyed by the fact that once again I had chosen something of two short and easy verses.
' I think so,' I said, trying to get the words straight in my head so I could start again.
'Not good enough', he snapped, 'You have had a whole week. You should know this like a parrot.' Learning like a parrot was one of his favourite ideas.
'I could sing it,' I offered in desperation.
'Don't be cheeky. You can learn two poems for next week. For now, just read this one from your book, and give it plenty of *expression.*'
'I've forgotten my book,' I admitted in a quavering whisper.
'What?' He was quite angry now. 'You fail to learn your poem, you are cheeky enough to say you will sing instead, and now you tell me you have forgotten your book. You know what this means.'

A sudden pang like a twist in my guts told me that I did know. I felt almost faint with terror, not just anticipating the pain but realising the humiliation, the catastrophic fall from grace. A pulse pounded in my head and tears sprang to my eyes. By now Mr. Fisher had the cane in his hand. He must have realised that his anger had pushed us into a situation neither of us wished. I had never before done anything worthy of punishment of any kind from him, even a telling-off, and here he was about to cane me. I held out a shaking hand, and he gently laid the tip of the cane in it like an offering.
'Two poems,' he said, and turned his back.

Somehow I complied with this instruction, and the threat of caning was never repeated. I managed it by resurrecting my pièce de resistance from babyhood, a more or less accurate rendition of Hilaire Belloc's story of Jim who was eaten by a Lion; ('There was a boy whose name was Jim. His friends were very good to him') putting plenty of expression into the tragic ending, 'But when he bent him over Jim, The honest keeper's eyes grew dim. The lion having reached his head, The miserable boy was dead.' I did not have a book with this in it, so I wrote it all out in my Composition book and told Mr. Fisher that my father had taught it to me that week. Inconsistencies between my version and Belloc's original were therefore glossed over. Annoyingly, he did not ask me for the second poem. Maybe he forgot.

This approach to the learning and appreciation of poetry did not kill my enjoyment of it. The Cullercoats Method of music teaching was a close-run thing however. I enjoyed singing, the hymns in assembly, or Geordie songs learned as we sat in large numbers on the hall floor. If only there had been no need to introduce us to the rudiments of musical theory. With no equipment whatsoever, Mr. Fisher attempted to teach us the difference between quavers, crochets and minims. We sat at our desks, left hand flat and palm upwards, the first two fingers of the right hand extended. By beating a rhythm with these two fingers on the palm of the hand we attempted to replicate strings of these notes drawn on the blackboard. A crochet was a single strike, accompanied by the word 'tah' spoken firmly. Two quavers were fitted into the same space of time, while saying 'tata'. A minim was the trickiest, the first beat performed exactly like a crochet, the second beat represented by holding the fingers away from the flat hand, while saying 'tah ah'. Thus, for example, the first line of Away in a Manger should be 'tah tah tah tata tah tah tata tah tah tah tah ah'. Needless to say, in our class of fifty-one, there were many who could not keep this up, several who did not want to, and a number bent on sabotage. Any resemblance to any aspect of music disappeared into a sound like a violent rainstorm on a tin roof. At the front of the classroom would be Mr. Fisher, attempting to conduct, at first with a pencil, then with the cane, his most frequent, frenzied, instruction being, "Stop! Stop!"

There was one lesson a week conducted by another teacher, Mrs. Andrews. This was when the boys were taken away to do dangerous manly things with saws, hammers and nails, the results of which appeared as misshapen letter racks, three-legged stools with sloping seats, and planks adorned with cup hooks. Meanwhile, we girls did sewing. The only useable article I can remember producing was a fabric envelope for holding the needlework, which was our first project. Mine was pink gingham, with my initials worked on the flap in blue chain stitch. After that we spent most of the time doing a rough version of embroidery, in case we ever had the opportunity to lead the life of a Victorian lady. We had large bodkins, coloured wools, and did our sewing on a material Mrs. Andrews referred to as 'crash'. I did not understand the use of the word, except that it was obvious the stuff was something of a disaster. Whatever she called it, it was indistinguishable from a piece of sacking. Nevertheless, with this unpromising stuff, we learned lazy daisies, french knots, satin stitch and chain stitch. On the edges of the fabric we practised methods of sewing already rendered obsolete by the Singer sewing machine. We turned double hems, tacking first then finishing with herringbone stitch. We made french seams, being told that this was the preferred method for joining slippery satin when, later in life, we would find ourselves making our own knickers. I knew with a clear certainty that I would never, ever, use this information, but felt differently about the embroidery stitches. My mother sometimes bought linen tray cloths from the Wool Shop at the bottom of Longston Avenue, and blue transfer outlines that were ironed onto the material to form a guideline for embroidering flowers. I liked doing this, although my skill never really developed beyond the lazy daisies with french knots for their centres, and chain stitch stems. I hated Mrs. Andrews. She was dumpy and irritable, and once made fun of my name. Mainly, though, it was because she taught a B class lower down the school, and I felt vaguely insulted that the girls had to make do with what was clearly an inferior teacher while the boys went off with Mr. Fisher.

This anachronistic harking back to past times had echoes in other lessons. The style of handwriting which we had been taught, and which I found so beautiful, was unchanged since probably a hundred years before. This also was tested on a weekly basis, competitively, as our carefully written pieces were displayed on the wall of the corridor for all to see. In this the star of our class was Jean, whose writing achieved a beautiful curved symmetry. I admired this, but I was quite pleased with my own. This was Jean's especial gift, I thought. She had her place in the second row of the class, so her skill did not frighten me.

In other strange ways our activities reflected the preoccupations of earlier times. We had to be kept fit in body as well as mind, and our timetable included a certain amount of exercising in the yard. I don't know what the boys did while the girls played netball (there wasn't space enough for football and we had no playing field) but boys and girls together did drill. This really was marching, with short poles like cricket stumps on our shoulders, up and down the yard in lines, following orders to halt, and right turn, and left wheel. Strangely, I enjoyed this. It was orderly and satisfying. I had a good sense of rhythm and co-ordination. Although I knew that soldiers did it, it seemed more like a type of dancing to me, not unlike the Eightsome Reels, Gay Gordons and Strip the Willow that we skipped through in the hall on wet days.

Probably, there was still a strong motivation in schools to turn out good little citizens of the Empire, shown to us as large areas of pink on maps of the world. Certainly we were given a notion of superiority that we had been fortunate enough to have been born British. In my case, it was a feeling that I clung to with a disproportionate sense of relief. Being British was an immutable thing; a way of being superior that did not involve hard work, anxiety, or the possibility of being found out to be a secret failure. I didn't find anything strange in Robert Louis Stevenson's poem (short, so I learned it once for Recitation):
'Little Indian, Sioux or Crow,
Frosty little Eskimo,
Little Turk or Japanee,
Oh don't you wish that you were me.'
The lesson had been moderated since the previous generation, maybe. My Aunt Hilda once told me that when she was at school, she was actually taught that Germans were arrogant, and could be recognised by the flat backs to their heads, Italians were dirty and the French untrustworthy. We weren't encouraged in such active xenophobia, but our opportunity to demonstrate our place in the world came with a special day in the Summer term.
'The twenty-fourth of May is Empire Day.
If we don't have a holiday we'll all run away,' we used to chant in the days leading up to it. The day's holiday did not mean absence from school, however. We put on an outdoor show to which our parents were invited. In part it was a Sports Day, with a few running races. The younger children danced around a maypole, invariably muddling their ribbons, falling over, and crying. Folk dances were a feature, the Scottish ones being my favourite, as I already had a kilt. The wet days in the hall meant that we had a wide repertoire of dances that we could perform, including old-fashioned ballroom dances such as the Veleta and Sir Roger de Coverley.

The whole event was presided over by one child, a girl dressed up as Britannia. She wore a long dress, a cardboard helmet painted gold, and held a big shield painted with the Union Jack. It appeared to be an important role, rather akin to being chosen as May Queen, but I never felt deprived or slighted at not being given the part. It was obvious that whoever sat on the high stool all afternoon could not be leading Strip the Willow, or winning the races, or singing Hills of the North Rejoice in the top class choir. I had much more opportunity to demonstrate my abilities, and therefore my right to maternal affection, in the thick of the activity. Besides, for two or three years I enjoyed the status conferred by the fact that Britannia wore a frock from my dressing up box, a relic of Auntie Lizzie's heyday, in ankle-length pink guipure lace with a fishtail train.

Perhaps the most important and obvious sign of my success at that time was my position as top class prefect. Prefects were drawn only from 4A, and there were about twenty of them. Each of the eight classes in the school had a boy prefect and a girl prefect of their own. The duties were mostly policing at playtimes, making sure the members of your allotted class went outside quickly. Then at the end of play, a bell was rung and each class lined up, a row of boys and a row of girls, ready to march back into the school. The two prefects patrolled the lines, ensuring silence. Clearly, the two who were chosen to oversee their own class, 4A, were deemed to have the respect of their classmates as well as Mr. Fisher and Mr. Freeman. I enjoyed the honour, and appreciated it, although I could see that it was only fair that someone who regularly inhabited that top left-hand desk should be so appointed. The 4A boy prefect was my friend Alec. When we were much younger we had made badges, pretending to be prefects, or members of the Famous Five, by picking the cork lining from fluted metal bottle caps, and sticking them onto our cardigans, the metal on the outside, the cork pushed in again on the inside. Now we had beautiful enamelled badges in the shape of a shield, the word PREFECT diagonally in gold against a maroon back-ground. I found it immensely comforting that there was some obvious, although unexplained, connection between the words PREFECT and PERFECT.

Further Training

It is 2002. I am sitting on a plastic chair at the side of a large high room in the Palais de Justice in the small Dordogne town of Riberac. One wall of the room, facing elegant high windows, is covered by a long mirror with a barre for ballet exercises. The old dappled surface of the mirror greenly reflects trees surrounding the market square. They move gently, breaking the yellow light of a hot morning. But I am not watching the trees, except as changing shadows that marble the shiny floor. Mostly, I am trying to keep the muscles of my face smooth and relaxed so that no one will notice the unstoppable stream of tears that flows over my cheeks. Surreptitiously, I catch them with the palm of my hand as they reach my chin.

I have been allowed the privilege, as I am her visiting grandmother, of staying to watch five-year-old Jasmine's ballet lesson. No other adults are present; the children slide in through the door to greet Madame, and their mothers depart for an hour. So here am I, already conspicuous by my presence, although Jasmine seems pleased rather than embarrassed that I have been allowed to stay. I must control my sentimental response to the sight of eight small girls, dressed in pink practice frocks and crossover cardigans, pointing their little feet and carefully raising their plump arms. Madame is a woman of about my age, but firmly muscled and lithe. Her legs in their smooth tights, and her neat round bottom, move strongly and gracefully. Her voice, slightly raised above the sound from her CD player, is firm, the stream of French blending and curving with the music, like a poem describing the movements of the children, rather than the instructions to instigate them. Jasmine is serious, her eyes on Madame's face. Although her understanding is good, French is not her first language, and she concentrates hard to follow the movements. I see her small face, the clear dark eyes, the smooth pink curve of the cheek, and the swing of her bright auburn hair. She is engrossed, her movements correct and rhythmical. Also, she is not ever going to be a ballerina. Already it is clear that she will be too tall, she is strong and athletic as much as graceful, and she is no extrovert.

I want to know what is in her mind. It is easy to assume that the surface involvement with the lesson, the compliance, even willingness, imply her enjoyment. It is easy to sink into one's own sentimentality, overcome by the appeal of the small rounded body, the innocence with which the little face is raised; easy to forget that the child is unaware of her own beauty. The turn of the arm, the spread hand, the way her bottom sticks out when she points her toe, all look unselfconscious. I really want to believe that what I see is also what is in Jasmine's mind, that for her too it is beautiful and simple, a pleasure for the moment. The danger exists that the pleasure of the watching adult is transferred to the child, and an assumption made that the pleasure is shared.

My anxiety is that her feelings may in any way echo my own as a small girl, when Saturday mornings were given over to the civilising influence of Mrs. Pascoe's dancing school. For me in those days, there was pleasure, but it was not unmixed. Another target had been applied to an activity that should have offered only enjoyment. I was to work hard at the exercises of ballet in the hope that it would improve my posture. Too much reading (heavens, the one pleasure that gave me access to so much of the material for work, knowledge, success and therefore love) had apparently made me round-shouldered. The possible faulty logic that had me holding up my head, tucking in my chin and dropping my shoulders seems to have gone like this. My mother liked the idea of my having lessons in ballet; scope for further accomplishment on my part, she perhaps hoped. Probably she also hoped I would enjoy it. However, it would be indulgent to do something purely for fun; it must have a worthy, improving purpose. Hence, the concentration on my bent back. The upshot was the impossibility of my saying I didn't want to go to the lessons; no use attempting to refuse the treat, until I had learned to stand up straight. In fact, although I did get some enjoyment from the lessons themselves, I felt a desperate need for some time off, some time that was not work. Getting up on Saturday mornings at the same time as school days, going through the same cold ritual of washing and dressing, hurrying to the station for the train to Monkseaton, was a chilly imposition.

In my memory those mornings were always autumn. There was a dismal chill in the air, and the street from the station was lined with large-boled trees dropping slimy rags of leaves onto the pavement. The ballet school was in one of the large Edwardian houses, where two ground floor rooms had been made into one. The space was bare, with a shiny linoleum floor, a mirror and barre, and a baby grand piano in one corner. Several years later, the lady who played this piano was the unwitting cause of an embarrassing surprise for me. My mother and I got onto the train to go to Newcastle one day, and as we made our way to our seats, my mother gave a cry of pleased recognition, 'Miss Hutchinson!' Turning to me, she said, 'You remember Miss Hutchinson.' I had no need to remember her, I saw her every day. Miss Hutchinson, as far as I was concerned, was my Latin teacher. My motherhurried to where Miss Hutchinson sat near us on the train. For a moment, I thought she looked oddly smaller, slightly prettier in a softened and blurred kind of way. Then I saw my Miss Hutchinson sitting opposite her. How odd that in my school career I should twice have been taught by one half of an identical pair. It occurred to me that I was a very unobservant child. Not only had I not noticed that the face at the front of my Latin lessons was the same as the one at the piano during the ballet lessons. I also had not noticed my mother making friends with one of them during the short breaks we had from the dancing exercises.

As she watched our lessons in 1950 or so, did my mother experience the surge of sentimental pleasure that impedes any empathy with the experience of the child? We, the dozen or so girls in the class, were dressed just as Jasmine, except that our tunics and cardigans were pale blue. We did not wear tights, and my legs always looked incongruously bruised above the crossed ribbons of my soft pink slippers. Our lesson was a little more formal than the one I saw in Riberac, with some emphasis on learning the classic positions of the hands and feet. 'Feet in first position… and point… and second… and point… and third.' There was French too, although I don't think I knew what that was. The words became part of a normal, but specialised, vocabulary, the pliés, the arabesques, the pas de chats.

Once a year, there was a display of our skills, staged at the Priory Theatre in Whitley Bay, a smallish wooden building smelling of damp and creosote, normally used by travelling repertory companies to put on a summer show for the holiday makers from Glasgow. It was exciting to wear the costumes, made in the weeks beforehand by our mothers, exciting to choose the correct colours of greasepaint makeup to show up in the stage lighting. For a while all the Saturday mornings seemed well spent. The tarantella dress, in rustling taffeta with coloured ribbons, the flowered hats and gypsy blouses, the way the piano below the front of the stage sounded echoingly loud, gave our little routines a glamour and importance. Once, I danced a solo to Dvorak's Humoresque, very nervous and shaking, until I realised that the audience were invisible beyond the lights. In the wings afterwards I was unexpectedly asked to take a bouquet to the lady playing the piano (not Miss Hutchinson), but because I could not see her beyond the brightness of the empty stage I refused and cried.

Another solo was performed by Miss Seymour, Mrs. Pascoe's younger assistant. For the first time, I saw pointe shoes and a proper tutu, and longed to reach that level of expertise. At the same time, a thought, which I could not have expressed at the time, told me why Miss Seymour was teaching little girls in Monkseaton rather than dancing in wonderful theatres in London or other impossibly faraway places. Something about her short figure balanced above the large toes of her shoes chimed in with my sense that the dancing made me feel ugly. My bruised and sturdy legs, mottled with cold, were never going to pirouette nimbly across the international stage.

As for Jasmine, I am encouraged that at the end of the lesson, after Madame has given balloons to all the children to thank them for their co-operation, she runs to me smiling and skipping, not doubting that I have enjoyed it. Surely that assumption of my pleasure arises from a certainty of her own.

So, if I was not to be a dancer, perhaps I could be a pianist. I admired my father's ability to play. This he did infrequently, but when required he could rattle out the songs from the News Chronicle Songbook, and carols at Christmas. When I brought home the music in order to learn my dances, he could open the book and launch into the tune without practice, which gave me the impression it must be easy. Then one evening I was invited by Valerie, a girl in my class who was briefly my best friend, to visit her uncle, who wore a coloured bow tie, and played boogie woogie. I was entranced, and metaphorically rolled up my sleeves, ready for the lessons with Mrs. Walton.

Everyone in the neighbourhood who had piano lessons went to Mrs. Walton. A rather severe-looking middle-aged widow with one almost grown-up son, she lived conveniently on the corner of Longston and

Houghton Avenues, a minute's walk away from home. My time was five o'clock on Monday, and the lesson lasted half an hour, the longest half-hour of the week, as it turned out. The routine did not vary; I would trudge out of our front door at five minutes to five, a shilling in my pocket to pay for the torture to come, and Invitation to the Piano under my arm. At two minutes to five, I would ring and enter, go into the gloomy back room to wait, and worry about lack of practice. At precisely five, the previous pupil could be heard to leave, and I would be called through to take my place at the shiny black piano. The room was actually quite pleasant and sunny, with a large bay window facing the street across the crazy-paved garden. In my memory, those afternoons were always sunny, and distantly I could hear other children playing in the street.

The upright piano stood against the wall opposite the window, and Mrs. Walton was installed, apparently permanently, on a straight chair to its left. She was equipped with a stubby baton and a bottle, like a small soda siphon, containing air freshener. The session always began with scales. In spite of three or four years of lessons, I never became fully comfortable with anything more complex than C major. The appearance of a sharp or a flat caused my heart to sink. Then I would stumble and struggle my way through the 'piece', supposedly practised during the previous week. Fixed in my mind was the notion that the use of the left hand was much more tricky than that of the right, and those dilatory digits would stumble out of sight onto the wrong notes while the tune progressed fairly well where I could see it under my right hand. Even had I put in the recommended half-hour daily, I could never have played through uninterrupted, because of my flopping wrists. Every so often, as I mangled the Blue Danube Waltz or Teddy Bear's Picnic, Mrs. Walton wielded the baton, not to conduct my faltering rhythm, but to strike my knuckles as a reminder to stop resting my hands on the keys. Then also she would give the lever on the bottle a few vigorous squeezes, and a cold mist smelling of lavender and clean toilets would drift down onto the backs of my hands.

Usually, it would not be suggested that I move on to the next piece in the book, as I had not reached the required standard. I feel sorry for Mrs. Walton now, but at the time the emotion she inspired was a mix of fear and boredom. Compared to the chaotic finger tapping of our lessons at school, my invitation to the piano should have been a pleasure, but I wasted it. Mrs. Walton's dogged persistence in the face of my lack of interest meant that I did learn to read the music on the page, although I could not translate it into appropriate sounds. Years later, when I realised that I could sing rather well, this was useful. I cannot explain why, at the time, my idleness was tolerated at home. Frequently I would be told that when I was older I would regret my inability to play, and indeed this turned out to be true. My mother's reaction to my lack of success was a sort of dismissive scorn, burdening me with the painful realisation that I had wasted an opportunity to earn approval and love.

Moving Up

There was a sense of coming change during the last term of our year with Mr. Fisher. Our surroundings began to feel dull, and somewhat outgrown, although I am sure I was not alone in secretly wishing that the time of familiarity and security did not have to end. For me, who had almost perfected the deceit that allowed me to be my mother's perfect child, the uncertainty of being able to maintain it in a more challenging environment made me nervous of the change.

Suddenly, an experience that threatened to shatter my carefully constructed image of achievement and status. I had invented a monogram of my initials, which pleased me by its symmetry. A rectangle divided horizontally, with a V shape in the upper half, incorporated the three letters EMH. I identified my pencil case, my ruler, my exercise books with this device neatly inscribed on sticky labels or scratched with the point of my compasses. During this time I had been reading a number of school stories, including the first part of David Copperfield, with the description of how the boys carved their names on a door. Somehow, leaving your mark in this way seemed to be simply an inherent part of school life. Not long before, our room had been refurnished with new desks in brightly varnished yellow wood. They seemed incongruous and unattractive, not fitting into the room as comfortably as our old double desks with their cast iron frames and ink-stained battered lids. Several children found that the varnish cracked under a thumbnail and could be peeled in tiny flakes. Others scratched initials, even whole names, onto the undersides of the lids. Without thinking for a moment about what I was doing, I carved my monogram neatly into the most visible place on the top corner of my desk lid.

If only Mr. Fisher had caned me, shouted at me, sent me to Mr. Freeman to be spoken to sternly. He found the offending carving, waited until after he had taken the afternoon register, then with everyone in the classroom waiting to begin the lesson, took away my prefect's badge.

As I felt myself falling into the abyss of failure, which for me meant that ultimate betrayal of my mother, the blood drained from me and I almost fainted. A strange grey curtain drifted and bubbled across my vision; I could feel that my sweating hands, gripping the sides of my seat, were shaking as if I were frozen.

"Why did you think you could damage school property in that way?" Mr. Fisher asked me in a flat, toneless voice. The fact that he was not openly angry and shouting felt more threatening. I knew that he recovered very quickly from bad temper. As I had not, in fact, thought about my actions at all, I could not answer this, and fell back on the shameful, cowardly excuse. "Lots of people have done it," I replied. He turned to the rest of the class. "Who else has defaced school property?" he asked, quietly. There was a brief pause, then, to my amazement, and overwhelming gratitude, several people raised their hands. The first was a white-faced Alec, who removed his own badge with the other hand, and put it on his desk. The stolid grim faces of my classmates told me that they were not owning up in the knowledge that they would be found out anyway, but because there was a code of solidarity, which recognised excessive punishment.

Mr. Fisher picked up Alec's badge. He chose two children, apparently randomly, to replace us. Alec's badge was given to Colin Henderson, a funny, popular boy who looked almost as upset to be receiving it. His hand was not up, certainly in his case because he had not carved his desk. My badge went to a girl who was quite new to he school, a thin red-haired Scots girl called Elizabeth. I knew for a fact that she had scratched the whole of her name on the inside of her desk lid, and as she took the badge she looked at me with an expression of pre-emptive hatred. I was too shocked to feel any need to betray her, and she turned her back. I noticed that she held the badge in her hand for several minutes, pinning it on only after the lesson was under way.

Elizabeth kept her badge for only a day. Of course, Mr. Fisher thoroughly inspected all the desks and discovered her deceit. He decided that for our remaining weeks, as the top class we did not need two prefects, and that Colin could keep us in order by himself. My punishment was mitigated; in his usual manner he attempted to withdraw from the initial extreme stance, by giving me a yellow prefect badge which carried the job of standing in the corridor after playtime as the classes filed into their rooms. Alec was given charge of the class lower down the school that had been Colin's. I would rather not have had the partial reinstatement (this way the whole school knew of my demotion), except that I still had a badge to wear at home. My father asked why the colour had changed, and I shrugged and said I had lost my red one. Fortunately, my brother, three and a half years younger and in the first junior class, seemed unaware of the relative status of prefects, and had nothing to say on the subject.

The almost ritualistic frequency of tests in Mr. Fisher's class was a useful preparation for the exams that were soon to come. Before moving on to the next stage of our education, we had to be sorted. This was to be done by a process with the politically incorrect name of the Grading Exam. Those children who were graded as part of the top twenty per cent in the borough would go to Tynemouth High School, the rest to Linskill School, the secondary modern. The thing that was modern about it was that it existed at all, it not being all that long since children who did not go to the High School stayed another year or so at their elementary schools, then left for good. This is what had happened to my mother.

I was not worried by tests, and remember the day of the Grading Exam as being rather enjoyable. There was the opportunity to write a story and do some arithmetic uninterrupted. In my mind's eye I still see my loopy writing curling across the page, and the neat sloping patterns of my long division sums. As well as these familiar things, there was another paper called intelligence tests. I had not seen problems like these before, but enjoyed the game-like nature of the tasks. 'Which picture is the odd one out? Which shape fits in the space? What number comes next? Make a word from the following letters.' I had no difficulty with the words and pictures. The numbers were a little trickier, but mostly susceptible to logic rather than mathematical knowledge. I finished the exam with no doubt that I had passed, and this was in fact the case. When the results came, I was charitably thrilled on behalf of one or two of my classmates, those who sat in the middle of the room and downwards, and for whom it had not been a foregone conclusion. In fact fifty of our fifty-one passed, a massive confirmation of

Mr. Fisher's skill as top class teacher.

The day of these results offered an opportunity for the system to torture our parents rather than ourselves. Those children who had passed the exam were allowed to go home straight away with the good news, those who had not (the reason being that they did not have any good news to pass on) had to remain at school. We were aware that some fathers even stayed away from work for the morning; mothers of course were at home anyway. The swimming club families took a bit of a risk, exposing themselves to a public declaration by arranging to be at the club, where we would go when released with the news. I think that year there was only myself and Pam and Tom (who went to a school in Tynemouth), and we all duly turned up just in time for our mothers to toast our success in coffee. How dreadful it must have been for those parents waiting at home for a child who did not arrive. Had their son or daughter been abducted en route, involved in an accident, or merely graded as unsatisfactory for the grammar school?

My own involvement with examinations was not yet over. Another target had been set up, another expectation that I could exceed the achievements of most of my peers. In Newcastle were several private schools for girls, each with its claim to superiority over the offerings of the grammar school, for reasons of social status, or religion, or academic excellence. My parents chose the one with the most stringent entry requirements, an exam, an interview, and if possible a wealthy and (at least) middle class family. Clearly, if I was to get in, the responsibility was all mine. I was unaware of the discussions that must have taken place between my parents concerning the fees; my father was quite poorly paid, and the little money brought in by my mother's hairdressing in the kitchen could not have made a significant contribution. I think they made the decision in the knowledge that it was possible to win scholarships and bursaries that paid or reduced the fees. Years later, Auntie Lizzie in her dotage irritated my mother a lot; the son of my father's cousin (Billy, a charming boy without the burden of academic expectation and in danger of failing the Grading Exam) was sent to a commercial college in Newcastle instead of the secondary modern. Auntie Lizzie paid at least part of the cost of this, and got it into her head that she had paid my school fees too.

Several girls from Mr. Fisher's class went to Newcastle to attempt the entrance exam. I felt I did not acquit myself very well. The maths paper was more difficult than anything I had been exposed to before, and although I knew I had answered correctly the sums that I did, I did not finish the paper. Then the opportunity to write at length, my forté, required a description of myself rather than a story, a topic that I found uninteresting. There was a passage of reading, I think about Queen Elizabeth I, and questions to answer. After a few days, a letter came requiring me to be interviewed by the head-mistress, Miss Belton, so it seemed I had performed well enough to carry me through to the next stage.

I remember little of that interview. Presumably I was nervous, which would tend to make me rather tongue-tied. Miss Belton seemed very old, I suppose approaching sixty, as she retired not long after this. She was small and hunched, only her head and shoulders showing above her desk, and the front of her white hair was stained yellow as a result of her chain-smoking. She set a bad example to her girls in this respect, but it was not one that she would tolerate anyone to follow, almost on pain of death, or at least expulsion. We talked about the Guides, which I had only just joined from Brownies, so knew little of, and probably other things. By this time, I believe my mother had retreated into an irritable acceptance that I had failed, as I was reporting nothing that suggested a performance that would result in financial assistance, without which I would not be able to take up a place. So the day that we were informed that I was offered a bursary that would reduce my fees to seventeen pounds a term was one of relief and euphoria.

The next morning at breakfast I attempted to explain that I did not want to go to that school. I knew that the reason was to do with fear, of so many strangers around me, of being one among girls who had sailed through the entrance requirements. I had seen some of them, girls who had already belonged to the school's Junior House, who knew each other, and had loud, posh voices. I knew already that I would not be able to keep up the deceit that made me the Cleverest Child. But as the only reason I could come up with, for my aversion to the idea, was that I would be unable to go to school on my bike, my objection was over-ruled. Back at school that day, it turned out that two other girls in my class had also been offered places at the school. One was Christine, who had often shared my first and second place desk, so this was no great surprise. Although she had never been a best friend, we got on well enough, and I was relieved not to be going alone. The other successful candidate was more of a surprise. Judith's place had always been somewhere in the middle of the room, as far as I can remember. Certainly she had never shared that important top left-hand corner. So there were to be three of us going from Cullercoats.

Once I had become resigned to the fact of my future school career, I began to look forward to it. I was less worried about losing contact with my friends in Cullercoats, as there would still be the Swimming Club, and Sandra and I were going together to the Guides, which would also continue. In its favour the new school had two features. One was that it was a girls' school, with forms instead of classes, and mine was to be the Upper Third; this sounded very like the schools in my story books, so I looked forward to japes and possibly adventures. The other was the length of the holidays. In the Summer we would have eight whole weeks away from school, two weeks at Christmas and Easter, and a week at every half term. It was perhaps a sadly negative reason for liking the idea of a new school, but the truth was that I felt constantly exhausted by the demands of my life. Not that anything had been difficult for me so far, but the emotional strain of trying to seem perfect when I knew full well that I was not, had become quite draining. I longed for time off, and a school that supplied fifteen weeks holiday a year had a great deal to recommend it.

Preparations began for this new phase. One day my mother and I went to Newcastle for the buying of the uniform, obtainable only in Fenwick's department store, the official suppliers. Most of it was a specific shade of yellowish brown, so items from any cheaper source would not do. The whole kit was so expensive that my parents had to accept, perhaps even solicit, help from Auntie Lizzie. Maybe this is where she gained the impression she had paid for my schooling. In fact, the cost of the uniform was equivalent to almost two years of school fees.

Uniform began at the skin and worked outwards. For the winter we had beige wool vests and brown knickers, cream silk square-necked blouses, brown serge gymslips, a brown cardigan or sweater with a gold band round the neck, a brown gabardine mac, a brown velour hat with a brim and a brown and gold striped scarf. We had to wear knee-length beige socks, and had two pairs of shoes, a pair of brown lace-ups for out of doors, and indoor shoes that were slightly less sturdy with a strap over the instep.

Summer uniform started with white vests, the same brown knickers, brown and white gingham frocks, a brown blazer with the school crest on the pocket, and a straw panama hat. We wore white ankle socks and our strap shoes for out of doors in summer. Because of the cost and the quality of these expensive garments, most of them were bought too big, in order to make them last. Some years ago, I was amused to see an almost identical uniform in a glass case in Leicester's Costume Museum. It dated from the nineteen twenties, but looked in excellent condition.

The wearing of the brown continued throughout the seven years at the school. The only change was that when girls entered the Lower Sixth, aged sixteen, the gym slip and square-necked blouse were replaced by a brown skirt, cream shirt and brown and gold tie.

Our shopping trip did not end with this array of everyday garments, however. There was also the equipment for various activities. I was a bit startled by the fact that we had to have a brown cotton overall for Science lessons, in case of damage to the gymslip by acid. Then there was the games kit. As well as the hockey stick and tennis racquet, there was the brown pleated divided skirt (mid thigh length) and yellow Aertex shirt, white skirt and shirt for tennis, brown nylon swimsuit and yellow rubber cap, brown long socks and hockey boots, white short socks and plimsolls. We even had to have a brown cotton drawstring bag in which to store our indoor shoes so as to avoid carrying them to school each day. My mother was caught between the excitement, the pride that people in the store would see her buying Central High School uniform for her daughter, panic at the cost, and some annoyance at this strangely specific colour. Being the competent dressmaker that she was, she could have sent me in a home-made collection had the material been available.

Other pieces of equipment appeared as gifts from various members of the family. My Grandma, obviously hoping that I would be some sort of linguist, bought me a set of Collins Gem Dictionaries, a useful English one, French, German and Latin ones, which I did use, Spanish, Italian and Greek, which I did not. Auntie Lizzie gave me a Platignum fountain pen, very smart with a marbled red and grey case and a gold nib. Mrs. Crow, by now nearly ninety, gave me a five pound note, so I bought a steel Ingersoll watch on a black leather strap, a good supply of coloured pencils, and an item I had not known existed, but which appeared on the school list, a mapping pen. All of this went into my new brown leather satchel with silver buckles and two straps to be worn symmetrically on the back. I was ready to go.

There followed a strangely lonely time of waiting. The children who were graded into Tynemouth High School or Linskill went off in their new dark green or navy blue uniforms, presumably nervous or excited, discovered their new surroundings and became accustomed to them. Instead of walking to John Street they got on their bikes or buses, met other children from different junior schools, and embarked on their new lives, whether happily or unhappily. I saw Sandra in her green outfit, which suited her pink and blonde colouring, but she seemed too busy to say much about the newness of school. It was during this time that she and I went to the juvenile court to tell how we had been shot on the tennis court, both in our new school clothes, although mine did not yet really belong to me. I had three weeks of belonging nowhere, my first experience of the longer summer holiday.

I remember one morning going to the Swimming Club, one of those early September days, when the sunlight is soft and hazy, the sky delicate and waiting for the later strength of the sun. No-one else was there, and although I wanted to swim, I wanted company more. Alone in the clubhouse, I hung my new blazer on a hook in the changing room, then sat and listened to the silence. The space was shadowy and gloomy, the wooden walls and floor barely lit by the soft sunlight through narrow high windows. On one side of the room were three cubicles, only used by the older ladies, in front of which hung ancient cotton curtains, hanging limp and still. In the space under the stairs was the stack of deck chairs, their bright striped fabric muted by years of sunlight and salt air. Everything was so familiar and comfortable to me, the slight clean fishy smell, the tiny motes of dust floating across the soft beam of light, the crunchy feeling of sand on the floor under my feet. But there was a difference in me, a tiny constant shudder, as if a mild electrical current of nervousness was passing through me. My blazer, hanging opposite me, was illuminated by the strengthening sun, and I had a sudden strong wish to move on and belong in the new clothes. The wearing of it before my time felt ill judged. I remembered how the previous year, when Pam and Jean, whose birthdays in October were a month before mine, got their new bicycles. I also had been promised one for my birthday, and my parents decided to give it to me early, so that I could have a few more weeks using it with my friends before the winter set in. Sensible and affectionate motives, but Pam and Jean decided that I had received the present early because I was spoiled, took umbrage, and would not play with me until the time of my birthday, and the bike was mine legitimately. Now, I knew that my mother's wish for me to be seen in the brown blazer was a signal of difference. It did not make people admire us or like us more. I suddenly wanted to make the move into the new school, the new life, to legitimise the blazer. People could then react as they wished, but the reaction would be to the real me, whoever that was, rather than a pretence.

When the first morning of school came, the season had made the turn into autumn. It was chilly and grey, more noticeable by the fact that I had to make an early start. I was to make the daily journey on the train from Cullercoats to Jesmond, a familiar route, but not one I had ever travelled alone. Of course, on this occasion I would have company too, for Christine, Judith and I had arranged to travel together. Judith, who lived furthest from the station, would walk to Christine's house, then they would meet me at the top of Mast Lane and we would walk the last hundred yards or so to the station together. Our train was at two minutes to eight, so to give us sufficient time we arranged to meet at quarter to the hour.

Wearing the whole kit, from vest outwards, with my satchel squarely on my back, I arrived at the meeting place five minutes early. Most of the road towards Christine's house was visible to me, so it was with increasing anxiety that I stared in that direction seeing no sign of two more brown-clad figures. Three slow minutes ticked by, watched almost by the second on my new Ingersoll watch. At sixteen minutes to eight, my teeth almost rattling with anxiety, I began to trot in the direction of Christine's home, willing them to appear round the corner. Fortunately it was not far, and shortly before ten to eight I was knocking on the door.

"They went ages ago", said Christine's mother airily. "Didn't they wait for you?"

Five minutes' sprint, my heart bounding in my chest from exertion and fear, my new clothes stuck to my body with sweat, took me tearing onto the station with a couple of minutes to spare. There were my supposed school friends, neat and apparently calm, waiting on the platform.

"You weren't there," they stated flatly, with no acknowledgement of the fact that they must have gone by almost ten minutes before the agreed time. I had no sympathy with their complaint that they had been waiting ages on the station. In fact I wanted nothing more to do with them, and only stayed beside them because my nervousness at being alone slightly outweighed my anger and disgust. Even if it had occurred to me that they too were scared, and had probably hurried on to the station in their own anxiety not to be late, I still would have hated them for those few terrified minutes that they had caused me.

On the train, the two of them sat side by side, and I took a seat alone behind them. At Whitley Bay station, a tiny, terrified-looking girl in an over-sized brown uniform got on the train. I caught her eye, twitched my face into a smile, and slid along the seat in an invitation for her to join me. At Monkseaton the arrival of two or three more nervous ones, and a number of older girls, whose uniform showed signs of wear and adaptation, made me realise that I could not possibly get lost. Christine and Judith were welcome to each other I decided; I did not need them. This new school was something else that I would find a way to manage on my own, or at least pretend to do so.

And Away

During my childhood, I was protected from the actuality and consequences of death, almost as if it did not happen. One by one, the old people at The Crest succumbed, but I saw little reaction, except of a practical nature. Uncle Willie was first. Having set up the home in which he would be surrounded by, and cared for by, his wife's family, he lived only three or four more years. His 'bad heart' caused him to be permanently in bed by the time I was six, so my last memories of him were of visiting the bedroom at the end of each Sunday visit, so that I could be given half a crown for my school bank. Then he was no longer there. Life at The Crest continued, unchanged except that Auntie Lizzie was now the senior member of the household. She demonstrated this in various ways, of course doing no housework, and taking Uncle Willie's place at the head of the table. I would be asked to read from the Sunday newspaper, I think The Observer. It was too large for me to hold up, so I would spread it on the floor and crouch over it. If Auntie Lizzie needed to cross the room during this procedure, she did not avoid the spread pages, but walked straight across. I always felt this was a measure of her importance.

She took over the giving of the half crown also, which reminds me of a very strange circumstance related to this. At Cullercoats Infants School (this was while it was still in the old building on John Street) children put money into the school bank on Monday mornings. The transaction was recorded on a folded card, and after morning assembly these cards and the cash in a cloth bag were taken round the corner to the Trustee Savings Bank on Station Road. I know this happened, because for a while it was my job to do this errand. Was it really a better world, in which a six-year-old child could be sent alone with a substantial amount of cash, or were those teachers astonishingly naïve? The situation was not greatly different a few years later, when my brother was in his first job, aged fifteen. He was the office boy for a large company of shipping agents in Newcastle. When a ship docked, a briefcase containing thousands of pounds in cash was chained to Kit's wrist, and he was sent to the ship, on foot and alone, to take the seamen's wages.

Next of the old people to depart was Mrs. Crow. Almost ninety years old, she seemed to become smaller and smaller, until she was only a tiny flushed face on the pillow of her large bed. I had never been in the habit of entering her bedroom, but after I had spent the money she gave me for equipment for my new school, I went in to show her the watch and the pencils I had bought. She was too preoccupied with dying to look at them. "Your Auntie's going," she whispered to me, almost as if telling a secret. I did not know how to reply, and she died that same night.

Within a few weeks Uncle Fred also disappeared, almost unnoticed by me. I had heard the word 'cancer' mentioned in the house, and he also stayed in bed. For so long he had been an almost immobile presence sitting at the corner of the kitchen table. Unable ever to play, or even walk with us around the garden because he said he had a bone in his leg, which I took to be a metaphor for tiredness, he did not surprise me by being unable to get out of bed. But his death came as a surprise. No-one told me, or made any comment of which I was aware, then on a Sunday afternoon, Auntie Lizzie and I took a walk together up the lonnen to Mr. Elwyn's farm to buy bantam's eggs. At the farmhouse door, Mrs. Elwyn spoke to Auntie Lizzie in a gentle commiserating tone, commenting on Fred's long illness, and Auntie Lizzie began to weep. Suddenly realising what had happened, I was shocked. I tried to put my arms around her (aged eleven I was almost as tall as she), but she quickly regained her composure and we walked home in silence.

So now, only Auntie Lizzie and my Grandma were left. Still the house was full of warmth for me; selfishly, I knew that my own interest in the place had always been centred on Grandma, although I was fond of Auntie Lizzie. After a while, my visits became shorter. As soon as tea was over, I went to the bus alone. There were two youth clubs that met on Sunday evenings, and my friends had become more interesting than my family.

For a year or two the only different feature was that Auntie Lizzie suddenly developed an interest in keeping healthy by going for long walks. Sometimes the two of us would take the bus down into Northumberland Square and walk from there through Tynemouth, out along the pier and back again. This brief period was a time when she and I were closest. She lived long enough to see my first child in 1967, but her last years were a sad descent into senility and dementia.

One Monday night in February, when I was fifteen, the phone rang when I was already in bed. I heard my mother answer it, and realised she was talking to my father's cousin, Peggy, who still lived close by The Crest. The conversation did not last long, and I heard my mother's voice in the dining room beneath me, and my father answering. Soon, he was taking a coat from the cupboard in the hall, and I heard the front door open and close quietly. My mother peeped round my door, saw I was awake, and came in. She sat on the side of my bed.

"Your dad's gone to The Crest," she said. " Your Grandma's been taken ill." There was a short pause, then she continued. "Actually she's dead, though I didn't say so to him. Peggy said it was very sudden."

I felt nothing much. The words hung in the air, almost as if I had imagined them. I was thinking to myself, 'Well, she was old, seventy-nine. Old people do die.' I said to my mother, "She was all right yesterday." We had all made our customary Sunday visit the day before, and I had stayed long enough to eat the usual supply of sandwiches, scones and cakes. I realised that my voice had a slightly petulant tone, as if to say that Grandma had tricked us by being fine one day and dead the next. I would have liked some warning.

"Auntie Lizzie told Peggy that she just went and sat down in the big chair in the kitchen, closed her eyes, and died, just like that. No pain, not a word. Dr. Scott came right away and said it was a sudden heart attack."

There seemed nothing more to be said. I had a vague feeling of pain that coalesced into one of anxiety about my father. Never one to display strong emotion overtly, how would he conduct himself in these circumstances. An hour or two later, wakeful, I heard his return, a quiet conversation, then slow footsteps on the stairs. My bedroom door slid open a few inches and he put his head round.

"Still awake?" he asked, in a normal tone.

"Yes," I replied. "How are you?" I realised that my not enquiring about Grandma gave him the message that I knew already that she was dead. He did not have the difficulty of passing on bad news.

"I'm all right," he answered, and withdrew his head.

Nothing in my routine changed that week. I knew a funeral would take place on Thursday, and I was frightened of going, not really on my own account, but because of perhaps being faced with the vulnerability of my parents. We had had no practice in the display of painful emotions; my skill was in hiding pain from them. It was a relief when I overheard my mother saying to a neighbour that it was easier for Kit and me to go to school as usual. The death had no reality for me.

During those days, I felt normal, and was unaware of behaving differently, so it was a shock when on the Thursday morning I realised that I had forgotten to do my Latin homework. Handing homework in for marking was done by putting the book on a shelf belonging to the appropriate teacher. I found myself standing in front of the shelves, empty-handed, and in front of me were half a dozen books containing the work in question. It suddenly seemed an excellent idea to take one of them, go to the library during break, copy it, and hand both books in at the end of break. Miss Hutchinson would not take the books until lunchtime, so no one would know. I took the top book; the rest of the plan went smoothly, and soon the two were back in the pile, one at the top and one at the bottom. I had made a few differences in the translation, to avert suspicion.

At the end of the Latin lesson, by which time Miss Hutchinson had already looked at our work, she asked me and Barbara, the girl whose book I had taken, to wait behind. Clearly, the similarities were suspicious, but Barbara's denial that we had in any way collaborated was so transparently innocent, that I must be the culprit. I was asked to wait outside the staff room at the end of school.

Maybe the anticipation of trouble was something of a final straw for me. The door of the staff room was at the end of a short wide corridor screened from view by the homework shelves. There was a small round table at one side and two chairs. I sat down to wait, and quite unexpectedly began to cry, silently but beyond control. A great vessel of tears within me burst, and poured from my eyes. In a few moments Miss Hutchinson arrived, but I was no longer remotely concerned about what she may have to say to me.

"Well, it was a stupid, dishonest thing to do," she said sternly, " but there is no need to be quite so upset." Clearly, the method of my misdeed needed no explanation. I had not been so clever and original in my dishonesty as I had thought.

"I'm not crying about that," I said through my tears, "My Grandma died on Monday, and I've only just realised." It sounded a stupid thing to say, but to my astonishment, she immediately softened into shocked sympathy.

"I had no idea," she said gently. "Why ever didn't we know?" A brief flash of horror passed through my mind as I saw that my grandmother's death was about to get me out of trouble. It felt a complete injustice, as I had been quite unaware that it had affected me until a few moments before. I wanted to be punished, I wanted to be given pages of unseen translation to do. This was an opportunity to make me pay for all those years of pretending to be something better than myself. I had taken Barbara's book, not because I had been distracted by grief, but because I was inefficient, disorganised, too lazy to keep abreast of my work. However, I was sent off home, still crying, the two friends who travelled with me on the train shocked and upset by my unstoppable tears. I had not told anyone what had happened on Monday, because it had not occurred to me that it was of interest. When I got home still weeping, my mother assumed it was normal for me to cry on the day of my grandmother's funeral, comforted me a little, then it was over.

Afterword

W hy does the story end there? In a way, because it is the end of the first chapter, although there will be no more chapters. Many things ended at that time, not least the time of the Cleverest Child. Once I was at the Central Newcastle High School, I took on a new and more difficult relationship with my mother. She still needed me to fill the role, but it was no longer possible to do it easily or truthfully. Most of the other girls were at least as clever as I, and several of them a good deal more so. In that environment I excelled in nothing. I sang well, but Margaret Beckham sang better. For a while, I swam the fastest, but Anna Kellock came from India and outstripped me. I wrote interesting stories, but creativity was less important than literary analysis. I had a badge for a while; I courted popularity by feigning a sophistication I did not have, claiming to know about boys, and make-up and fashion, and was voted form captain for a couple of terms. But soon the other girls saw through this, ceased to value it, and my reign was brief. So, my mother pretended, and I allowed her to do so, while always feeling her nervousness that the pretence would collapse. The brown uniform was her talisman. As long as I could wear it, she could rely on it.

Remarkably, I became good at pranks and naughtiness, escaping to the ladies' toilet on Jesmond station at lunchtimes in order to smoke, or in

R.E. lessons wearing a false hairpiece in the neck of my blouse, to look like a hairy chest. When beehive hairstyles were fashionable, I prepared for school on the train by back-combing my long hair into two horns like a Viking helmet. Later, I took an unsuitable boy to the sixth form dance, and he got drunk (by going out to a nearby pub, of course; there was no alcohol in the school) and kissed the headmistress during the Bradford Barn Dance.

Life continued, I did what was expected, went to Nottingham University, got a decent degree in English, taught in secondary schools for nearly thirty years, got married, had children, waited until they were grown up, got divorced, married again. Now my time and my life are my own, I garden, and paint, and listen to music. Also, I write, the one thing that the Clever Child was really good at, but now I do it for me, for love of it.

Mostly, the story ended in 1957 because that was the end of the Past. After that, my father got a car, we watched television, the horses disappeared from the streets. From 1957 onwards I lived in the same world that I recognise now. Of course, change has continued. When I went to university, I paid nothing, the government gave me nearly enough money to live on. I had to be in my hall of residence by 10.30 at night, and no man was allowed in my room after 8.30. No-one was allowed to go home during term-time without permission. Clearly, many things have changed, and some have not. I taught for a while at Loughborough High School surrounded by the girls and lessons and smells and uniforms that I recognised from long ago. However, someone else has said, the past is another country, and for me the crossing of the border occurred in 1957.